Converting the Baptized

A Survival Manual for Parents, Teachers, and Pastors

WILLIAM J. O'MALLEY, S.J.

TABOR
PUBLISHING
Allen, Texas

Book design and cover design: Tricia Legault

Send all inquiries to:
Tabor Publishing
One DLM Park
Allen, Texas 75002

Printed in the United States of America

ISBN 1-55924-490-9

1 2 3 4 5   94 93 92 91 90

For
BOB GROENEWOLD, S.J.
and
JACK ALEXANDER, S.J.
who have been my brothers.

Contents

Acknowledgments

The following chapters first appeared in *America:* "Selling Faith to Skeptics," September 3–10, 1988 (Best Article 1989, Catholic Press Association); "Explaining Today to Yesterday," October 21, 1989; "Converting the Baptized," September 30, 1989; "Teenage Spirituality," April 29, 1989; "Toward an Adult Spirituality," November 18, 1989; "Jesus, the Warm Fuzzy," March 15, 1986 (reprinted in *The Catholic Digest,* April 1987); "Scripture from Scratch," February 4, 1989; "Mass and Teenagers," October 8, 1988; "Teenagers and . . . You-Know-What," April 15, 1989; "The Journey to Justice," July 15–22, 1989; "Fathering an Adolescent Boy," June 4, 1988; "P. T. Barnum and the Catechetical Quest," October 10, 1987; "Making Parents Apostles" (originally titled "Parents Are Apostles"), January 20, 1990.

The following chapters first appeared in *The Living Light:* "In Praise of Doubt," January 1988; "Good Guilt / Bad Guilt," October 1987.

"Faith and Imagination" first appeared as "A Leap into Light," in *Commonweal,* March 10, 1989. Copyright © 1989 by *Commonweal.* Reprinted by permission.

"The Adult Christian" first appeared as "If Mother Church Doesn't Let Kids Grow Up . . . Tick, Tick, Tick," in *The National Catholic Reporter,* March 6, 1987. Reprinted by permission of the National Catholic Reporter, P.O. Box 419281, Kansas City, MO 64141.

INTRODUCTION

Matchmaker, Matchmaker

Once upon a time, or so the story goes, in a great city not unlike Toronto, a priest slowly became aware that the man sharing the elevator with him was Groucho Marx. He finally cleared his throat and said, "Excuse me, Mr. Marx. I don't want to intrude. I had to thank you for the joy you've given people all these years." Without missing a beat, Groucho looked up under those eyebrows and said, "Wish I could say the same for you fellas."

Parents and teachers and pastors who are worried over the disinterest—if not downright hostility—the young show for things religious could well take that story to heart. Clare Booth Luce said that when she was thinking of converting to Catholicism, she kept looking at Catholics she knew, especially priests and religious, and she said in her mind, "You tell me you've found the truth. Well, the truth should set you free, give you joy. Can I *see* your freedom? Can I *feel* your joy?"

The premise of this book is that the young people in our schools and pews and homes have been baptized, but—except in a few rare cases—haven't yet been converted. If you don't start there, you might as well be speaking Mandarin.

No matter what our claims about the richness of a spiritual life or the rewards of organized religion or the need to study theology, what we do shouts so loudly the young can't hear what we say. An analogy pops up often throughout the following pages: Parents and teachers and pastors are salespeople, and the best salespeople are the men and women who not only are hot for their product but are using the product themselves with obvious results. The young people we love and teach are looking over our product, which has a great deal of powerful opposition. Their act of faith in what we offer can only be freely given; we can't compel it as we can (sometimes) compel external compliance. We are matchmakers. So our pitch better be damn good. Not just in our eyes. In theirs.

What follows is the result of twenty plus years of teaching religious education—mostly in high school but also in college and adult education courses. Most of my experience comes from working with a text called *Meeting the Living God* (Paulist), a course in epistemology and apologetics focusing on the existence and nature of God. The course has a notebook of reflections paralleling the text, and the students are free to say whatever they want without penalty—short of threats on my life.

Over that span of years I'd estimate I've read and commented on about 140,000 pages of young people's reflections on the basics of religion. (*The Guinness Book of Records,* take note.) Thus, I'm quite sure I have a sense of what youngsters honestly feel and think and believe, beneath the surface "cool" or shyness or seemingly unreachable distance. Most often, their sincerity has been palpable; most often, their problems are as simple as understanding words in a different sense from their parents.

But their most basic problem is that they have never undergone a conversion experience, and thus they see no inner benefit to themselves from religion—other than the almost completely external motivations of either pleasing their parents or avoiding a hassle with them. Many young people who asked me to witness their marriages were asking a priest, not because they cared about Mass, but to please or avoid hurting their parents.

Now, maybe the last twenty plus years haven't made me as red-hot a salesman as Bruce Barton or Og Mandino, but I think I'm pretty good at my trade. I've seen the swing from the orgy of righteousness in the late sixties all the way round to the jostling for the nonpassing lane to the MBA in the eighties—where the orgies are relegated to the weekend concert and beer and maybe some grass. In that time, I've also directed sixty-five plays, so I've been with the kids and seen their behavior with one another on a common job shifting in twenty years, especially in the choruses for big musicals, from a hearty involvement and camaraderie to a kind of indolent aloofness, enduring, in order to go to the cast party. And I've had to adapt my pitch again. And again.

Therefore, this book treats the audience: their skepticism, their fear of being hoaxed still again, their resignation to the likelihood that nobody can really do very much to change anything. Unlike other books, however, this one praises that doubt—first of all, because that is where our youngsters *are,* and second, because their very doubts are a healthy sign that they are now hungry for something more convincing than answers that satisfied children. Their doubt serves our mission, provided we're not afraid of it, provided we have faith in the good-heartedness and sincerity of our own children.

The book considers strategies to bring youngsters and Christianity together, in terms the *kids* find valuable, because the strategies don't begin from where almost all approaches begin—from the top down, from what we adults "know" to be the truth—but from the bottom up, from where young people are, from their (unreasoned) antagonisms.

As these pages do not hesitate to repeat, our job as parents, teachers, and pastors is to render ourselves unnecessary, to lead our youngsters out of a childish belief and practice into an adult belief and practice, so that they needn't face adult life with childish answers and they needn't run to someone else to solve their problems.

First, we must convince them—by experience of it—of the richness of the awesome presence of God all around them and within them. Without that, their religious education remains as academic—and irrelevant, to them— as history. Then we have to show them ways to solve their own doubts, resolve their own moral dilemmas, using the Scriptures and the library and prayer. They are going to leave the nest; perhaps they will even leave religious practice for a while. We have to give them the means to find their way back.

But let us all remember—and accept—our real mandate. Like Jesus with his first Christian school, his Twelve, we are not training sheep. We are recruiting and educating shepherds.

PART ONE

Human Fulfillment

ONE

Selling Faith to Skeptics

"Twelve years my kid was in Catholic schools! Now he doesn't even go to Mass. There's ten grand down the tubes." Maybe. Maybe not. You can take the boy or girl out of the Church, but you can't take the Church out of the boy or girl.

To my mind, the greatest problem such harried parents have is forgetting the very real distinction between having a personal relationship with God and having a personal relationship with the Church. Jews, Muslims, and even the unchurched have a relationship with God, ranging from the almost indifferent to the ecstatic, but they are not Catholic. Still, they are very, very good human beings and in some cases saints. It is interesting to note that one of the greatest practitioners of Christianity in our century was not a Catholic but a Hindu.

If I had children, I would very much want them to remain Catholics, but if they chose otherwise, I think I'd be willing to settle for their being saints. I think I'd even rather have them good human beings than grudging Catholics. And the choice, after all, however self-impoverishing, would be theirs and not mine.

In order to explain the Kingdom of God to the young—and to ourselves—we have to resort to metaphors, just as Jesus did. The trouble arises when we get locked into the metaphor and leave behind the reality we're trying to explain. This happens, without our realizing, when the word *Church* automatically triggers the idea of "them," rather than "us." It happens often when people say, "When is the Church going to do something about the boring Mass?" or "Why is the Church so unbending about birth control?" Quite obviously, the speaker is focusing the word *Church* to only the institutional Church, and even more tightly to the pope and the Vatican, since the people in the pews are in no position to have an effective say in liturgical change and, if the polls are correct, the majority of that "Church" has chosen a position on birth control quite opposite to the official Church's.

Admittedly, one has to continue to pay dues at a country club to remain a member, and one would think a Catholic would have to reaffirm the commitments of his or her baptism at the Eucharist at least frequently (if not weekly) to be considered still a member. But one's baptism doesn't disappear after so many Masses missed.

We are not talking about a club when we speak of the Kingdom of God; we are talking about a family—the daughters and sons of God. The norm of membership is not the paying of dues. Even if the son never writes home, even if the daughter ignores the needs of her parents, they are still members of the family, however prodigal. The nonpracticing Catholic has not left the Church any more than such a son or daughter can leave the family. In the image used by One who knows, they are not ex-members; they are strays.

Let us be rid of those clubby, institutional, corporate images, which Jesus never used, and which seem to imply that if one does not attend Mass, he or she is no longer in the family. God created saints for thousands of years before Baptism or Mass or the Church itself existed, and grace is not given on a "Members Only" basis.

However, hearing that, many youngsters reply, "Great! If good non-Catholics can make it without Mass, so can I!" And "make it" usually means merely avoiding hell, which they're none too sure of either, and which in any case is way, way in the future. Which shows that they, too, have limited themselves to institutional images of the Christian community: dues, meetings, memorized rules, exclusivity, blackballing. Young people who make that kind of statement are not really convinced Christians at all but rather pagans with the Christian label peeling off.

The reason is that all of us who try to pass on the faith find the institutional metaphor easier to deal with—as do our listeners—than the seemingly more "airy" images of People of God, Body of Christ, Kingdom of God. As a result, our task seems to be to get their bodies into church, rather than getting the Church into their hearts.

With that institutional metaphor central to our understanding of the Church, it is no wonder that a great deal of fretting has arisen from the disappearance of *uniformity.* There was a day (which only those over forty remember) when all priests gave the same doctrine and the same penances, when you could go to any church anywhere in the world and hear exactly the same Mass. Outside the home, the primary focus of one's identity was the neighborhood and the parish. It was clear-cut, simple, and reassuringly certain.

The self-delusive flaw in that nostalgia is that you can't go home again. Even the prodigal son returned to a new situation. We can't recreate the Church of 1948 or the Church of A.D. 48, because the world in which the People of God must now work has changed beyond recognition since the disciplined and frugal days after World War II. If Booth Tarkington wrote *Seventeen* today, he'd have to call it *Ten.* The people we are offering the faith to in our religious education courses now are a politely skeptical group of youngsters, who feel they've been bamboozled once too often—by their parents, presidents, and popes, among others. As a result, from puberty onward, a teenager's greatest fear is being "uncool," taken in, hoaxed. And one has problems getting a skeptic to make an act of faith.

Orthodoxy is easier in an insulated ghetto. But when our Founder sent us out into the world, he sent us out to cope with pluralism. Since the morning of Pentecost, the Church has forsworn the cozy security of the Upper Room.

❝ The nonpracticing Catholic has not left the Church any more than . . . a son or daughter can leave the family. ❞

In the deghettoized, pluralistic society to which we are missioned, one's act of faith in Christ and his Church must be freely and autonomously chosen, or else it cannot survive the assault of so many other powerful and contrary points of view. One cannot survive a dorm debate at NYU or Berkeley with nothing more than an uncritically memorized and accepted catechism of answers. If born-again Christians have a better chance in that hostile arena, it is not their memorized chapters-and-verses but the manifest joy and enthusiasm of their lives and their love for Jesus—which we quite obviously have not managed to inject into the hearts of our own young.

Whatever brings back our "strays," it must be as powerful—to *them*—as the countless hours those same children have been taught by the media to covet, beginning before they were able to read. Is the love we ourselves show for Jesus and the Church as powerful as that?

It is foolish to blame this softness with pluralism on Vatican II. We can "blame" only our Founder, who sent us out into the uncomfortably diverse highways and hedges, and on Saint Paul, who was comfortable with "Jew or Greek, male or female, slave or free." As long as one has owned the heart of the gospel, everything can be discussed, even—as Paul proved at least twice with Peter—the strictures of religious law we thought for a long time were nonnegotiable, like circumcision and dietary rules.

But our most basic error is that we forget we are offering religious education to young people who are baptized—but who have never been converted.

Knowing about God vs. Knowing God

It is more important to know God than to know about God. Surely the Curé of Ars and Joan of Arc are evidence enough of that. And yet we tell youngsters all about God for twelve years and rarely show ways the youngsters can meet this elusive and, to them, mostly academic "Subject."

Then we assume, since the "Subject" has been explained so often, that the young understand It, accept It, and will remember It. Such enviable naiveté flies directly in the face of every teacher's experience. Moreover, what adult can still rattle off the seven gifts of the Holy Ghost, or the cardinal sins, or any other catechism answers after the first two or three? Nor did memorizing the catechism daunt Adolf Hitler or James Joyce or Fidel Castro. What kept us in the Church was not catechism answers; it was felt faith and hope and love—and need.

The answer is not in mere knowledge; the answer is in understanding. There are two very different strategies at work in our religious education programs trying to achieve knowledge and understanding, each of which has its advantages and liabilities. In the first strategy, the child's interests, questions, and receptivities dictate the matter. In the second strategy, the matter is primary, and although the teacher tries to relate it to the child's needs, knowledge of the matter comes first.

The first strategy's strength lies in its immediacy and relevance; its weakness is that it sometimes fails to open up students to a wider horizon, which is precisely what "conversion" means. The second strategy's strength lies in its clarity and its complete coverage of religious topics; its weakness is that children "learn" the matter whether they find it meaningful enough to remember or not.

On the one hand, there is a value in films, collages, and discussions. But it can be deceptive. It can go on too long, long after the time when youngsters need some solid data and some solid logic. Discussions can be a mere pooling of ignorance or a way to "one-up" the teacher. We go in their door—and stay there. In short, entertaining without challenging.

On the other hand, there can be a value in academic theology, apologetics, and even to some extent memorizing. The theological illiteracy of our young today is appalling. But theology, too, can be deceptive. It can begin far too early, as if the use of reason actually did click on at age seven. Sophomores will yawn over material that seniors will be truly enthusiastic about. ("Why didn't they tell us this before?" "We did; you yawned.") What's more, it can be as unrelated to everyday life decisions as math or history. In short, bloodless.

Concretely, what can we do? Collages and films have their place in religious education—in elementary school and in ever-decreasing doses afterward. In the latter years of elementary school, by all means let there be memory of a catechism—but stripped to the barest essentials, not mere incomprehensible exam fodder. What purpose is served in children befuddled by the Trinity, or the Virgin

Birth, or simony, or hell? What would Jesus have told children—and just as important: when?

Finally, from the beginning, let us engage our children in retreats and methods of prayer geared to their receptivities. It is not primarily club members we are training—or even theologians; it is saints. Our primary goal is not mere cognition but the transformation of what being human can mean, the opening of horizons, in a word: conversion.

Theology Is an Adult Endeavor

It is a painful fact that just when young people are ready to begin a serious study of theology, they stop formal religious education. Just at the time they become intellectually capable and even willing to cope with nuance and detail in mathematics and literature, they leave religious studies behind in high school and go on to study more and more complex mathematics and literature. This is one reason why so many adults and even older priests are heartsick over the lack of uniformity in the Church: because the last time many of them learned anything new about theology was back in college or the seminary or even in high school.

Susceptibility to reasoning begins for most young people sometime in high school—usually by junior year. Perhaps it's a growing awareness of the SATs and college; perhaps it's also puberty and dating, the real internalized discovery of others as persons like themselves, for the first time. At that stage, the threshold of their response noticeably begins to deepen toward a more adult level of honest confrontation with the data. Further, in other subjects they are beginning to deal with a more complex logic: trigonometry, chemistry, sociology, and so forth. Why not in religious education? To keep youngsters at the "let's see a film and discuss it" level may be far easier on a teacher's preparation and grading time, but it is both distrustful and wasteful of good minds. Moreover, it will take only one quick-witted atheist prof in college to undercut those twelve years.

A Spectrum of Doctrines

One obstacle to cooperation between the so-called Right and Left in the Church over religious education is, I think, the refusal of the Right to agree that doctrine is not a monolith but a spectrum.

❝ Our primary goal is not mere cognition but the transformation of what being human can mean . . . in a word: conversion. ❞

Surely there are nonnegotiables, to deny which is to deny the essence of Christianity itself: the divinity of Jesus, our sharing of the divine aliveness (grace), the real enlivening presence of Christ in the Eucharist, the fact of the resurrection, the call to serve the needy, and so forth. But there are also doctrines, mostly disciplinary, of hardly any importance at all: when we should stand and sit at Mass, whether women should wear hats in church, removing Saint Christopher from the calendar of saints, and so forth. Between these two extremes lie matters whose importance ranges from the weighty to the trivial.

We cannot put our minds in neutral and say that every pronouncement from the Vatican has equal weight. This would be a kind of "creeping infallibility" that sees not only every word of the pope but every word of a bishop or priest or nun as beyond question, thus denying the indisputable fact that God gave us minds before seeing the need to give us the magisterium, or even the Ten

Commandments. Even Vatican I and Pius IX didn't mean that.

I have found one of the greatest impediments to securing the gospel and the Church a fair hearing is the issue of birth control. Smart young people can't understand why the Church, rather than frustrate the function of an ovary, would rather frustrate a whole person. The same young people would agree with the Church's stands on abortion, war, the Third World, and yet they take that stance on artificial birth control and—with total illogic—use it as the one weak spot that brings down the whole house of cards. That's sad, but anyone who wants to teach religion to youngsters has to realize what an obstacle it is.

Furthermore, let us be clear that faith is neither a commitment made after every doubt has been laid to rest nor a commitment without the slightest shred of evidence. Faith is both calculated and a risk. Even physics—the "hardest" of sciences—guarantees only a high degree of probability: trustworthy but not unimprovable. Faith is not certain knowledge; it is a well-researched bet. And anyone who makes a bet without some doubt is either brainless or owns the casino.

But year after year students have told me they thought doubt over the pronouncements of the Church was some kind of sin. Where did they get that idea? Perhaps from those of us who argued too definitively. Perhaps from those of us unwilling to share our own doubts, which nonetheless have not cracked open our faith. Perhaps from those who, without realizing, give the impression that our intelligence is less a gift from God than the decrees of the magisterium.

The Essentials

What follows is not a syllabus. Nor is it in sequential order on a four-year scale. It merely attempts to give a rough outline that might help departments assess the thoroughness of their own curricula and might help parents narrow the baffling scope of religious education to a manageable size. It is far less comprehensive than the new Catechetical Directory and, for that reason, perhaps more practicable.

What Is Human Fulfillment? What will make me happy and worthwhile as a human being? The media say money, fame, sex, and power will do the job; how do I know they're wrong? What answers to that can I find in psychology, materialism, communism, atheism, non-Christian religions, Christianity? How should I judge the success or failure of a human life: mine?

Is There a God? If the answer to that question is no, then all religions, all theologies, all scriptures are self-delusive trash. What would be the consequences to my individual life if there were no God? What would it be like to live a few years, and die, and cease to be real forever? What evidence is there for me to trust in God's existence? Is science really in opposition to religion? What are the consequences to my life and my behavior if there is, indeed, a God? What would be my indebtedness to such a Being?

What Is God Like? Who has known and can tell me about God? Why should I accept the Hebrew and Christian Scriptures as a privileged self-communication of God? If Scripture, like the language, symbols, and myths of Shakespeare, is so dense and foreign to me, how can I learn to read it without a teacher? How can I learn to understand what God is saying in Scripture to me personally?

How Can I Relate to God Personally? Alone in prayer? Through communal prayer and worship? Through response to the needs of my neighbors?

Why an Organized Church? What are the advantages? What are the limits of my obligation to this community and its authorities? Do the sacraments work some real internal change in me and my relationships—even if I don't feel any different? Why can't I confess my sins directly to God without a priest? Why should I go to Mass so often? What can I do if my parish doesn't seem to offer me meaningful worship?

> **66** *Faith is not certain knowledge; it is a well-researched bet.* **99**

How Does Belief in God Change My Relationships?
Why do human beings, including myself, do evil things? As a Christian, what obligations do I have to share my limited time and funds with the needy? If God is good, why would God create a world where there is so much suffering? What role does sexuality really play in God's idea of human fulfillment? How do I identify a moral problem honestly, search for legitimate moral options, and assess those options honestly in the light of the Church's teachings, and come to a personal decision about it—not as a child, not with a teacher or priest, but as a mature adult?

Until youngsters have at least temporarily satisfying answers to those questions, it makes no difference if they know the dates of Nicea or can knock the socks off a teacher with an explanation of *homoousios*. And that ten grand will, indeed, be down the tubes.

The job of every religious educator—including parents and pastors—is to render themselves unnecessary, so that their young will go on learning, worshiping, and serving, even when they are out on their own. When we demythologized hell, we tossed away the ace of trump. No great loss. But we did leave ourselves a job: to evangelize not only our children's minds but also their hearts. If we want to convert them, we can no longer use fear. Only love. And joy.

Perhaps then youngsters could make, for the first time, their own act of faith—instead of a vague trust that their parents or the Church or "everybody" must know what they're talking about. Perhaps then they might see that going to Mass is not a matter of obligation but a matter of gratitude. Perhaps then our young might be in danger of genuine conversion.

And now it is time for me to get to the task of answering those questions.

TWO

"Proving" Yourself

Once upon a time, long, long ago, when wishing still made a difference, Little Red Ridinghood and Hansel and Gretel and Jack and the Goosegirl all set off on their various adventures. It's still happening today, except their names are Meghan and Gary and Michelle and Dwayne. The only reason we have libraries is that, no matter how styles change, fundamental human nature never does. Since time immemorial, adolescence has been a quest. And no matter whether the hair is shoulder length or flattop, or the skirts are Mother Hubbard or mini, the Grail is always the same: Who am I supposed to be?

Only the brave and imaginative few set off on that quest. Most, like the majority of their biddable elders, take refuge at the center of the herd, where they are less likely to be noticed or surprised or criticized. Whoever's at the font of the pack surely must know where we're all headed. "Of course," you have to go to school, and then college, and then find a job, and have a family, and a house, and . . . well . . . "succeed." The answer to the Grail question is obvious: I'm supposed to be like everybody else.

Only the remarkable few have the courage—or persnick-etiness—to pull out of the herd and ask that most humanizing of questions: Why?

When I ask students why they are not working up to potential (and they are many), the almost invariant response is: "I guess I'm just lazy." Nothing further from the truth. The young have an enviably bottomless supply of energy—as witness any school yard during recess or any Friday night dance. What they lack is not energy but motivation: an internalized realization *why* any rational being would want to know French idioms or how to factor a quadratic equation—some understanding of a real connection between what they endure every day in class and "success." And the final goal is just, well, whatever's next. More. Somebody sets up these obstacle courses by which you "prove" yourself worthy to go on to the next. To them, the daily grind is as purposeless as Psyche sorting seeds.

There is a radical difference between schooling and education and between good instructors and good teachers (which ought to include all parents). Good instructors strive for precisely what we have now: indoctrination to "the way the System works"—docility, ingestion of arbitrary data, predictability, patience with dull routine, and "proper" behavior. On the contrary, good teachers are subversives, cattle rustlers, guerrillas. They are not at all irritated when their well-planned class gets sidetracked by kids raising their hands, risking being counted. Minds over "the matter." They want to seduce as many as possible to forsake the sterile security of the herd and set out on the lonely quest that makes one's life a story worth telling.

Unfortunately, most kids try to "prove" themselves—validate their parents' expenditure of care, time, and money—by *external* yardsticks, simply because those are the only gauges they've been given. School, athletics, looks, clothes, cars, sex—all ways to say to others (but not genuinely to oneself): *"See!"*

Young people have always been told, explicitly or wordlessly, "Why don't you grow up?" Till recently, that meant act like an adult, take responsibility for what you do and say. Now, primarily because of the media, acting grown-up is more important—and more externally measurable—than being adult. If you can drink, drive at night, and have sex, what further need have we of testimony? Most kids know by junior year where you can buy "proof."

❝ Most kids try to 'prove' themselves . . . by external yardsticks, simply because those are the only gauges they've been given. ❞

But there is another factor that works against a youngster's evolving an adult self, one that I have never seen mentioned in studies of adolescents. Ironically— perversely—this barrier to self-acceptance arises from a most salutary motive on the part of parents and teachers: inculcation of the virtue of humility, but uncorrected by its opposite: pride. When students write a reaction paper on what they're proudest of, they almost invariably smoke-screen for a paragraph or so and then begin: "I don't mean to be conceited, but . . ."

There is, I believe, a profound effect in the young person from that seemingly simple and trivial mischoice of words. It is not pride that goeth before the fall; it's arrogance, *hubris.* Not only is there nothing wrong with being rightly proud of a job well done, but there is also an absolute need for pride if the youngster is to develop the positive self-image that enables her or him to strive for even more. Genuine pride is aware of its shortcomings but not shackled by them. Arrogance, on the other hand, is vain about aspects of the self for which the individual can take no credit: looks, family background, brains. It is smug in its own unexamined certitudes; it is adept at backbiting, faultfinding, and sneering; it never feels the need for confession or compassion. It was arrogance, not genuine pride, that brought down Adam and Eve, Oedipus, the prodigal son, Faust, Raskolnikov, Hitler—the Nietzschean *hubris* that says to the gods—and to everyone else: "I am above you. I don't need you."

Every year, there are always a few students who truly need the narcissistic starch taken out of them. But they are very few. By far the most are fine young people fumbling around in the dark for the Grail. Too many, though, have been convinced—by report cards, fumbled passes, and the mirror—that they're "nobody special." Deceptively pious reading of the words "unprofitable servants" becomes a self-fulfilling prophecy. Whenever I've finished hearing a confession, I always say, "Well. You're a good person, aren't you?" Rarely has anyone responded with a simple, forthright "Yes. Thank you." Most often, it's hedged with a qualifier like, "I hope so," or "I try to be," or "Oh, well . . ." They never seem to have heard that bad people don't come to confession; only good people do.

In the nonreligious domain, the young have resurrected the stance on personal acceptability associated with the stern, Pelagian and Jansenist moral theology many of us remember from our long-lost youth, in which justice stood guard on love, and candidates for the priesthood were examined on their ability to ask the right canny questions to show that the penitent could not be absolved. That demon, exorcised by Vatican II and its *sequelae,* has returned sevenfold, and the diabolic demands for self-distaste no longer cry from the pulpit and confessional but from the tube and billboards and pages of slick magazines. You still have to answer a lot of questions and clear a lot of hoops to prove yourself worthy of even a skeptical and highly tenuous absolution and acceptance. And there are myriad shortcomings you haven't even examined yet, but of which the Torquemadas and Father Arnalls of Madison Avenue will soon find ways to make you aware.

If you don't think very highly of the vehicle, it's not likely to take you very far. And surely you're not likely to take off on any quixotic pursuit of something as elusive and unmarketable as a Grail.

What we owe our young is confidence—a word rooted in *"fides"*: faith, a faith anchored not only in God, or one's parents, or in the American way, or in external yardsticks, but in one's self. Any young man or woman with genuine confidence, justified pride, will not settle for "the gentleman's 70," does not hesitate to step in when novice sadists are tormenting some poor wimp, will not cheat or lie when he or she is cornered, cannot be demeaned by racial slurs, will not fall for, "Honey, if you really loved me, you'd let me do it."

It is true that each individual must wrestle alone for his or her own soul—a self, character, conscience, personally validated ethic—which are all words for the same reality. But some young people have a head start, because they have a confidence grounded in the wordless certitude that their parents love them, without any need to prove themselves worthy of it. An experienced teacher can tell in a snap which kids those are, by their serenity, their easygoing humor, their dependability. Quite often, such youngsters are the ones who not only "succeed" but are more easily seduced from the herd and onto the quest, because they feel no need to "prove" themselves. Any test or challenge they encounter is not a way to prove themselves but a way to *im*prove themselves.

But in my experience, the majority of young people at least sense that there are a few riders that make being loved or even being accepted—even by their own parents—conditional. Rarely do young people hear, flat out, "Oh, you'll never be worth a damn!" but it is not unheard of. More often, the expectations are wordless and quite indirect—and most often without the parents' having the slightest intention of belittling the child or any realization of what the youngster is actually hearing. "Oh, your father is such a failure, and your sister is such a disappointment to me," which the sensitive translate into, "If you don't succeed, you won't be loved, either." Or: "We've sacrificed so much for you, but it's all worth it, because we know you'll make us proud someday." No matter how quickly the parent says that, the child always hears a very long, wistful pause before "someday," and even without the pause, the clear implication is that the parent has insufficient evidence to be proud yet. Not what was intended, but quite often what is heard.

I base my conviction of the diminished self-esteem of too many youngsters on the fact that any criticism of perfectionism *invariably* triggers a brouhaha in class. "Ya gotta give 110 percent!" This quite often from a boy with a fine mind and a C average; he means on the football field and "when you get out into the real world." Twenty-seven years of that consistency, in three high schools and two colleges, convince me that too many youngsters don't believe that anything they do is quite good enough. There is not the slightest whisper of a danger that those kids might become arrogant; their perfectionism is a built-in governor even against legitimate pride.

I've been there myself, far more overdramatically than most kids suffer it, but it will serve as a "worst case scenario."

When I was a kid, I was no jock; I proved myself with grades; whatever sense of self-worth I had was rooted exclusively in those report cards. Although that made me the immediate first target in every grade school dodgeball game, it was close to cause for canonization at home, where Dad had only finished high school and Mom had never finished grammar school. At a Jesuit high school, I never once got below a 90. In college, things slipped a bit, but then when I entered the Jesuit seminary— "competing" against *la crème de la crème*—it became one slow slide into the Slough of Despond.

For the seven years of philosophy and theology, the "power" courses were almost all taught in Latin, from Latin textbooks, and there was only a single exam each year on all the material of the year. An oral. In Latin. Grades were on a ten-point scale: 10, *summa cum laude;* 9, *magna cum laude;* 8, *cum laude;* 7, *mediocritas.* Now, in Latin, *mediocritas* means "average," but it doesn't have quite that cheerily bland glow in English. Then, 6, *non superat mediocritatem:* "He is not able to achieve mediocrity"; 5 meant you failed and went into a less taxing track.

❝ What we owe our young is confidence—a word rooted in 'fides': faith, a faith anchored not only in God . . . but in one's self. ❞

All my life, grades had been my self-validation, and I thought, wrongly, that grades were the way you proved yourself worthy of being called "Jesuit." I'd written and directed and starred in plays; I had loads of wonderful friends; I'd even published a few things. But it wouldn't have mattered if I'd been produced on Broadway and my friends hugged me every day and told me I was the sweetest snooky-ookums on earth. Because, for six years, my grades—my indicators of self-worth—were: 7, 6, 7, 7, 6, 5.

It would actually have been easier if I could have convinced myself that my earlier academic achievement had been a fluke, and that I was just genuinely dumb. But all the other minor successes indicated that I wasn't all *that* dumb. I worked with enough concentration and devotion to shame a workaholic Buddhist. But it wasn't enough. My best hope was *mediocritas.* If that. I became irritable, quicksanded in self-pity, roving the corridors like the

Hound of the Baskervilles looking for affirmation. Finally, I was quite seriously tempted to suicide.

So I saw the long-suffering spiritual father, over and over again, and he said, "Well, if you feel that way, you shouldn't be ordained. At least not this year." Back and forth I swung, tormented, till finally one day in January, I came out of his office, still in stupid anguish. Everybody was going in to lunch, but I couldn't stand to be with people, so I went back to my room, and paced, and fretted, till finally I couldn't stand it anymore. So I lay down, trying to fall asleep, trying to escape.

But I didn't fall asleep. The only way I can describe what happened is that, suddenly, it was like drowning in light. I was surer than I've ever been in my life that I was in the presence of God. And I was accepted. Unconditionally. The only way I know how long it lasted was that it was two hours later when I became aware of time again. And I sat up, and I said: "I'm a good man!" Without any hedges or demurrers or need for clarification. "I'm a good man. And I'll be a good priest. Because I'm a good man!" I grabbed my ice skates and went down to the deserted lake, and I skated around in huge circles, and I shouted it out into the silvery silence: "I'm a good man! And I don't need *anybody* to tell me anymore!"

It was the most liberating moment of my life. And it's never left me. Now, when I sin—and surely I do—I know that it's a good, dumb man who did it, worth picking up and starting over. Now, when I confront injustice, I speak up, because all that's needed for the triumph of injustice is that good people be silent. Now, when I have ideas I believe worth sharing, I do, even though some will surely think me an apostate or a grandstander or just a plain damn fool.

And from that moment on, the five proofs of Saint Thomas Aquinas became as unnecessary as my appendix.

That moment is also the reason I'm irredeemably a teacher—so that the kids I teach won't have to wait thirty-

26

two years, as I did, to realize that they're good. And it
caps my certitude that too many of the youngsters I teach
are frustrated perfectionists (which is redundant), because
every time I tell them that story, you can read it in their
eyes: they understand.

It is also why I would rather teach theology to the
young than do anything else—except perhaps give
forgiveness and the Eucharist, because so much of our
self-worth is tied up with our image of God.

There are some few teenagers who believe God an
irrelevance, and it's part of my job to ask them to stand
at the coffin of a seventeen-year-old, or visit a home for
retarded children, or squat in a foxhole with tracers an
inch above their butts, and come back and tell me the
question of God is irrelevant. And if God is irrelevant,
what relevance could *I* possibly hope for?

There are some few airy atheists, and their unexamined certitude can be at least shaken by a protracted study
of novels and plays that probe human suffering and the
problem of evil. Probably most effective is Samuel
Beckett's *Waiting for Godot,* the perfect distillation of the
airless hopelessness of atheism. If there is no God, then
Mother Teresa and a Times Square pimp get exactly the
same reward: annihilation. That says something about our
long-range value, no matter what others or we think of
ourselves: we are all, objectively, just so much potential
garbage waiting to be picked up. Possible. But sobering.

By far the majority of the young I teach have at least
some vague, unfocused belief in a God "out there
somewhere." Both through analysis of the universe and
Scripture and through centering prayer exercises, I have
to try to make them see that God is also "in here," too,
and try to correct the hazy image they have of God—and,
therefore, of themselves in relation to God.

Few—if any—still have the image of God many of us
had when we were their age: the hatchet-faced Puritan
who's makin' a list and checkin' it twice and just *waiting*

for us to take one . . . false . . . step. And yet that image of the vengeful God is lurking there somewhere in their subconscious, despite what's happened to religious education in the last thirty years. When you describe that image of God, even with the most lurid overacting, their laughter is just a tad pinched and nervous.

---

66 *Too many youngsters don't believe that anything they do is quite good enough.* **99**

Judging from three thousand plus responses, far more see God as George Burns, a pixieish, senile benevolence, usually good for a touch, willing to live and let live. Or as Vonnegut's prophet, Bokonon: "Live by the *foma* [harmless untruths] that make you brave and kind and healthy and happy." That image is certainly supported by an approach to God in education, homilies, and church art which I've belabored elsewhere in these pages as Jesus, the Warm Fuzzy. Surely a good corrective to the Hanging Judge, but it overcompensates, to the point where many young people write that God will forgive anything if you just wish you hadn't done it.

Far better, I think, to ask them to consider God as embodied by Jesus and understood by Paul, and Luther, and Tillich. Jesus never asked the adulterous woman for species and number; the father of the prodigal never asked for an accounting of every last farthing. But before the forgiveness could become effective, they did have to come home, not because God is a stickler for formality, but because the sinner needs to ask for and hear the forgiveness. Paul shows, again and again, that we cannot justify ourselves before some accountant God who keeps score of every peccadillo and good deed. Luther and Tillich tell us that the greatest burden—especially for good, humble

Christians truly striving to do their best—is to accept *being* accepted.

We serve a God to whom we *cannot* "prove" ourselves. Because there is no need! God loves us *before* we can merit such love. God loves us as a mother loves her baby, before the baby can do anything to deserve her love, before the mother has even seen the child. When we sin, God loves us as a mother still loves a child in prison. Because both are helpless to do otherwise. That's the way they both are made.

Like the futility of perfectionism, that is a difficult concept for young people to understand unselfishly: "If God loves you no matter what, then why be good?"— because anyone who treated someone that generous so selfishly would be a pretty mean-spirited SOB. Even when they understand it rightly, it is difficult for them to accept, especially if they have been wordlessly, unconsciously, constantly trained to ferret out flaws and cherish every external—if fleeting—validation. But we have no other choice. It's the truth.

Once anyone has accepted that God, that Incomprehensible Generosity, and accepted the bewildering fact that God has chosen each of us "out of the no of all nothing," that our sins are important only if we refuse to come home, then we've got a candidate for the quest. Then we have a potential apostle.

There is, of course, a catch. Confidence has a price, because—in a sheepfold—anyone with confidence is going to look arrogant. Then again, who with any brains would give a tinker's damn about criticism from sheep?

THREE

Explaining Today to Yesterday

Across the subway aisle perched this little sixty-plus lady. Grandma Walton. She clutched her bags, eyes darting as unobtrusively as possible—right, left, right—like a sparrow in a falcon roost. Her dearest wish seemed simply to skitter into her apartment and triple-lock her door. Then the car door rumbled open, and a big black boy with a two-hundred-watt smile pimp-rolled in and sat right next to her. Under a corona of gold chains, his chest bulged from a leather vest over a shirt exhorting us all to "Party Naked," all gathered under a flattop Eddie Murphy hat and shades. And he carried his blaster box like a maternity nurse. Well, that ol' box was squalling some message incoherent to me, to Grandma Walton, to those around us cloistered mutely behind the *Daily News,* but the boy's nodding head, snapping fingers, and beatific grin showed the message was not only loud but clear and much to his liking. Us? We weren't even there.

The lady grasped her packages more defensively and pursed her lips just short of implosion. "*Sa*-vage!" she finally rasped and rose into the protective anonymity of the straphangers.

If I can use the word *old* about a lady just a tad older than myself, that little old lady was right. He *was* a savage. Not because he was black, or wore chains, or denied the humanity of the rest of us in the car. I've taught white boys in Brooks Brothers' blazers who were as self-protectively indifferent. The boy with the box was a human being who was still about 92 percent animal, becoming less and less humanizable by the day. He protects himself from loneliness and confusion and frustration and other people's expectations with noise; so do the suburbanites. He wears a "uniform" to declare his "cool" aloofness from the very madding crowd; so do they: not merely Brooks Brothers, but Woodsman Chic, Motorcycle Mode, Heavy Metal Storm-Trooper-in-Drag. He's resolved that he's not gonna be hurt or even bothered anymore; so have they. The young at least seem "savages," according to the Eisenhower nostalgia of the little old lady. And me. Only difference is that the Brooks Brothers kids have yielded to the surface rules, and the boy with the box refuses.

On the other hand, perhaps because of twenty-seven years "in the bush," I might be a touch more immune to the defensive secretions they spray at us to say, "Get off my back!" I can pass among them now almost as one of themselves, yet maintaining my aloof, benign bwana image. The noise of the blaster box really bothered me, too. But something redeemed inside me liked that boy. The way he walked, what he wore, what his recordings wailed—all said, "Take *that!*" But how could I explain that to the little lady who'd called him "Savage"?

Haven't we all felt, with the mad prophet in *Network,* like throwing up the window and shouting to the world, "I'm mad as *hell,* and I'm not gonna *take* it anymore!" Odd. The little lady and the husky boy were saying *exactly* the same thing: You're intruding on my space! Get outta my face!

31

We are all reacting defensively to the same "society"—media, government, crowds, litter, noise, "them." But in different ways. Neither the lady nor the boy can afford the relative insulation of the suburbs. So she yields to the phobia, like Woody Allen: "They're all out to get me"; the boy acts counterphobically, like G. Gordon Liddy: "Hey, man, how 'bout you drop dead?"

The young are a puzzlement to those of us who believe we grew up in Grovers Corners, just down the road from "The Waltons," when things were "as they should be": lean and straight-backed once-for-all-married parents, children patched and starched and dutiful, dependable neighbors, and no sirens. Now, in exchange for the dubious advances of plastic, space shuttles, and twenty-four-hour-a-day entertainment, we have girls with makeup as garish as hookers, boys with earrings and otherworldly haircuts, and the inevitable Walkman. Like going to bed in *Our Town* and waking up in *A Clockwork Orange.*

Like the ozone layer, the superego of our society has been eroded bit by bit, so slowly that we didn't even notice. And the result is the same as the erosion of the civilized veneer from the boys who were abandoned on the desert island in *Lord of the Flies.* Beneath the stuffy choir robes there hides a painted savage, and beneath the Eton caps there seethes a reptilian brain stem. I would not say, with Golding, Luther, Calvin, Voltaire, that human beings are no more than beasts lurking under masks of pseudo-civility, that we are merely a higher and more complex form of animal. But I do believe we are not born fully human but only humanizable.

I do not mean a baby is not human. As Chesterton said, the most primitive human being could draw a picture of a reindeer, but the most fully evolved reindeer can't draw a picture of a human being. The difference between an animal cub and a human child is the same as between a marble and an acorn. You can plant both the marble and the acorn, but the acorn will grow into an oak and the marble will just lie there. It doesn't have the potential to be anything other than what it is; the acorn does. So with the human baby: a healthy little animal—untroubled by thought or doubts, contentedly eating, excreting, exploring, and sleeping. Undiluted hubris. But the baby has the potential for far more, not merely knowledge but some measure of understanding, developing not merely his or her mind but his or her soul. Only human beings are capable of becoming not only creatures but creators.

---

66 *Like the ozone layer, the superego of our society has been eroded bit by bit, so slowly that we didn't even notice.* 99

But just as the acorn can drop into leeched soil, or among rocks or thorns, the child can grow up stunted. Many of today's young grow up in ghettoes, impoverished of challenge or praise or dignity—without which full humanity becomes not unachievable but very, very difficult. But the suburban young can also be stunted, by their very affluence, overprotected by doting parents who don't want their children to wade through the crap they endured at that age—which, again, deprives them of precisely the challenge that leads to fuller humanity. Both rich and poor children are humanly impoverished. What's more, both poor and rich children endure the same commercial inducements to infantile greed, the same brain-numbing programs, the same dull, overly efficient and utilitarian education. They have a certain unnerving truth when they say, "You were *never* my age." Since we faced the trauma of adolescence, the important has been trivialized (death, sex, love), and the trivial has become important (athletics, physical appearance, the peccadillos of prominent personalities).

We are not talking Penrod and Sam here, or even Holden Caulfield. We're talking Alice in Wonderland, topsy-turvy time, where almost overnight—or at least without our realizing—the villains have become the heroes and the good guys are dweebs, geeks, and nerds. Heavy Metal groups achieve overnight success when they say they've made a pact with the devil, and Ozzie Osbourne wowed them by biting the head off a rat. (Fortunately, as always, the natures of things won out; he got rabies.) Many of us not born into this wonderland can't decipher the lyrics of most rock songs, but put on a pair of dark glasses and buy a copy of *Hit Parader.* It doesn't (couldn't) publish the really hard lyrics, but those it does will suffice: "She was good, ya know what I mean? . . . I'd rather laugh with sinners than cry with saints. . . . Turn around, bitch, I got a use for you. . . . You took it all too serious; I guess it had to end." Can't quite picture Grandma Walton crooning those over her mandolin, but sure has a stronger appeal to the animal in us than "Be Not Afraid" or "We Are One in the Spirit."

When *Gone with the Wind* first came out, it got a "Condemned" rating for a while, and housewives like my mother confessed it when they found out, even though they knew there wasn't the slightest provocation to sin in a man carrying his wife upstairs in one scene and her waking up like a pampered kitten next morning. Now, in the privacy of their own homes, our young can see films that make *Lady Chatterley's Lover* look like *A Date with Judy.* They have not only heard of but witnessed more murder, rape, and gore than a lifetime veteran in the army of Genghis Khan. Even their Saturday morning cartoons are an inducement to believe that it's a jungle out there and only the fittest survive. Savages? What else would one expect? The miracle is that so many turn out so well. Our families and schools are doing a better job than their critics might admit.

The young don't have the same bulwarks of certitude we had. In all the questions I've asked young people over the years, I don't sense they have any fear of the bomb; they don't even have any felt realization of death. But unlike ourselves at that age, they know they can't walk a couple of miles home from the movies. At least half of them can't be sure their parents will still be married next week or that the priest who counsels them to chastity is not seducing little children. Were we ever cynical enough even to dream that Roosevelt or Truman or Eisenhower was a liar and an unindicted coconspirator—or that they could become millionaires from it and have their advice sought by world leaders once again? Or that they could smile away our selling arms to people responsible for holding a dozen Americans hostage? Did we ever hear our parents make derogatory remarks about the pope? We grew up in a world where someone who followed a religious vocation was held in admiration; our children grow up in a world in which even many parents think such a person must have a mental circuit unsoldered. "You were *never* my age."

But the young are not without certitudes, some of them almost impenetrable. Their most basic conviction is that success means laying permanent hold on money, fame, sex, and power. And because they don't have them, they feel powerless, inadequate, frustrated— unsuccessful. What's more, they've gotten enough report cards to know in their gut that most of them will never have them—not in the undeniable measure of those who make it onto "The Tonight Show Starring Johnny Carson." That's one of the main reasons, I believe, for senioritis, when seniors' minds go into a stall. Students who, till now, have done at least respectably, slowly settle down to get the maximum result from the minimum input. The students themselves tell me that they've put in three and a half years, and now they deserve a break. Hardly convincing. Tell that to your boss three and a half years into your job. They do have a strong point when they say that nothing they study is going to be of any use to them "out there," because it won't. Everything they've read in the newspapers and seen on TV convinces them that image is more important than substance, that it's not what but who you know that counts. But there's a heavy contradiction when kids still say they believe "you need an education to get a good job," and then refuse to do the work they have to do in order to get an education.

---

66 [The young's] most basic conviction is that success means laying permanent hold on money, fame, sex, and power. 99

My hunch is that the senior stall occurs because students are afraid. Come September, it's all over. It's get-serious time. Because college is the Big Sifter that decides whether you're going to be a lawyer or a salesperson or a gas-pump jockey. That is, whether you're going to be a success.

The painful irony is that they have children's minds in adult bodies. They really want to "get it all over at once," to "arrive." (Cf. Adam and Eve.) They can drive at night; they can drink; they can have sex—just like the real people on TV and in the movies and songs. But they're not free. They're still shackled to their parents' bank accounts, discipline, and expectations. And shackles chafe. That's the unreasonable frustration they try to drown out with the omnipresent Walkman. But where did that irrational need come from? At least I can't remember being that eager to be grown-up at that age. Nor do I sense a kind of Huck Finn innocence in their expectations of human beings and human life. Like Willy Loman's son, Biff, Huck just wanted to get out into the open with his shirt off. My growing fear is that many of the young I teach have embraced precisely the goals and values that destroyed Biff's father.

For a great part of their lives young people have been led to believe, like Willy Loman, that they should become "somebody" to be a success, and that the unspoken content of the word *success* is money-fame-sex-power. But in the first place, they can get those now only in small and unsatisfying doses. In the second, it's quite likely they might never get them. And in the third, as we all know, money-fame-sex-power—by themselves—simply can't deliver human fulfillment, no matter how large a dosage you get.

Every year, *The World Almanac* sends out researchers to shopping malls all over the country to ask youngsters who their heroes are. In 1989, it was Eddie Murphy; in 1988, it was Tom Cruise. (The smartest woman was Dr. Ruth Westheimer, which also has its insight into the minds of the young; of the suggested qualities for a hero, "articulate" finished dead last.) At least the characters both Murphy and Cruise play are hip, sexy, unencumbered, invulnerable, self-enclosed, "cool." That's "the way to be." "Cool" is a mask of indifference: get outta my face, buzz off, drop dead. And if one wonders why so many of the young seem aimless, uncommitted, self-absorbed, and insensitive to others, there may be a clue there.

But the young didn't make themselves that way. "We" did: the all-pervasive ethos of monopoly capitalism which we've all not only accepted but gratefully embraced. It's been good to all of us, allowed us to give our children all those things we never had, made us the richest nation with the highest life-style on the planet. When I ask my own classes who their heroes are, the name that comes up most consistently is Donald Trump. In the minds of most of the young I've taught, "capitalist" and "American" are synonyms. In fact, making even the slightest criticism of capitalism in a middle-class school calls forth angry barrages and suggestions that the speaker might be a subversive. The speaker most certainly is; he is trying to challenge a deified economy with humanity—and perhaps even Christianity.

It is painfully trite to lay the blame on the principal agents of the economy: the media. And yet truisms are such simply because they *are* true. Arguably, electronic communication is the most powerful invention of humankind; unarguably, it is the most acceptably addictive. It's like those free buses to the casinos in Atlantic City. Or credit cards. It has changed the whole way a family interacts with one another. It takes hold of children's minds, even before they know they have minds, and tells them what's important; it forms their values and convictions more relentlessly and more cunningly than their parents and all the teachers they ever have will ever be capable of. It convinces them that all human situations are problems and should be capable of solution within an hour. It is the primary source of all assertions justified by "everybody knows" and "everybody does it." In order to appeal to the broadest possible audience, it has to appeal to the least common denominator, what all of us have in common, from the president of Harvard to that kid with the blaster box: pride, covetousness, lust, anger, gluttony, envy, and sloth. The animal. The savage. Just take a look at Geraldo and Morton Downey and Doctor Ruth. And which of us wouldn't like a controlling interest in the *National Enquirer?*

Someone once said that *Life* was a magazine for people who can't read, and *Time* was a magazine for people who can't think. Television and the stereo and the Walkman have assured us of a generation the majority of whom can do neither. Nearly a third of the citizens in the most prosperous nation on earth are incapable of reading a recipe or directions on a prescription label or the side of a Wheaties box. But every last one of them has an opinion on abortion and welfare and what life is for.

Hard to blame the media. They're only giving us what we want. If love, joy, peace, patience, benignity, goodness,

mildness, long-suffering, and fear of the Lord made a
profit, they'd give us those. If people are dumb enough
and lazy enough and addicted enough to play three-card
monte with their children's minds, who's going to arrest
the dealers? The basic tenet of monopoly capitalism and
advertising is: Unstinting pursuit of self-interest is the
best way to fulfill the public interest. True, within the
insulated limits of economics itself. True, provided
society—human beings—can legitimately be treated as no
more than competitors and consumers. But we don't need
recourse to Charles Dickens or even to the gospel to show
that unchecked self-interest is not in the public interest
and human beings are not merely economic factors. All
we have to look at is the suicide and drug statistics for
affluent young people, and street crime, and the SAT
scores, and one million teenage pregnancies a year—
400,000 of them aborted. Not only doesn't it work, but it
has a lethal effect on the human soul—on what makes us
more than animals or savages. We live in a moral ecology
in which, when one segment of the web profits unduly,
another pays unduly, and eventually wreaks its revenge
on the whole ecology.

> ❝ *[Electronic communication] has*
> *changed the whole way a family*
> *interacts with one another.* ❞

All I've written so far I believe to be true, at least in
varying degrees, of the majority of American kids. But if
all I've written so far is true, it makes me really scared.
And nobody else seems to be. How do I talk the Fortune
500 and the advertisers of America and the unions out of
engendering greed, when without greed they—and we—
would deflate back to the Waltons? Say I do throw up

my window and yell, "I'm mad as hell and I'm not gonna take it anymore." What do I do then?

It's useless to write your senator or representative. All you'll get is an offprint of the *Congressional Record*. Even a newsworthy lobby like Tipper Gore's against lecherous lyrics is laughed off, though there is at least some satisfaction in being an annoyance to the brain-washers and in having the sense that one at least tried. Boycotts have possibility, but organizing one would take the greater part of the rest of one's life. An individual would be far better advised to become a literacy volunteer or a foster grandparent; take just one or two kids to a play, a museum, the zoo. And listen; for God's sake, listen. Father Flanagan of Boys Town was right: there's no such thing as a bad boy or girl. They are animals only in the herd—or when connected by the Walkman to the jungle music. Cut one or two out of the herd, and they're just kids. Humanizable.

The most likely place to start is the schools. Any fight to raise teachers' salaries and make teaching a more honorable profession than penology is a blow to all those gloomy statistics above. Any demand to beef up (or even begin) the art and music departments, to make the school musical as appealing as the football team, to recruit every student into some kind of service project is an investment in kids' souls. Any expenditure to make the humanities more intriguing is a step closer to humanity for that boy with the box.

In October 1957, the Soviet launching of Sputnik spurred remarkable increases in U.S. science education funds, a project called, appropriately, the National Defense Education Act. One small canister started all that rolling. Then one might wonder why the enormity of all the stories in the newspapers and all the statistics does not move us to defend ourselves and our children once again. From ourselves.

PART TWO

Relationship with God

FOUR

Faith and Imagination

Faith is Greg Louganis. Or at least he's one of the best recent embodiments of faith I know. Who could count the dives that man has made in his life? Then, one time—one freak, impossible, unpredictable time—he cracked his head and crashed. But he got his stitches. And he climbed that ladder again. And he soared out into the terrifying emptiness. That's faith.

I give a test every year. One of the true-false items is: "Faith is a blind leap in the dark." Of forty-five high school seniors, supposedly safely brainwashed to Catholicism for well over a decade, thirty-five answered "true." Why was I surprised? It's happened every year for the last twenty-five, both with high school and college and adult students—just as those same students have consistently answered "true" to "Morality changes from culture to culture."

Some secret inner masochism must impel me to ask those questions year after year. But I keep wondering where they got the idea that religion is sheerly relative, dependent on the whim of the individual, not rooted in evidence which doesn't change from age to age. I can't blame their previous teachers, since in quite a few cases I was their previous teacher! But they cling like martyrs to that conviction. I rant and rave; I put on the chalkboard demonstrations worthy of Aristotle or Aquinas or "Sesame Street." But on the *fifth* test of the year, they're still writing "true" to "Faith is a blind leap in the dark."

Perhaps it happens because their parents, at the end of their patience, have so often snapped, "because I *said* so," or "because it's a mortal sin and you'll go to hell!" The youngster sees no logical connection between the punishment and the crime, and therefore there is none. There is the taproot of all faith problems: the epistemological problem, the difference between what *is* objectively true and what I—or some particular culture—*perceives* as true and uses as the basis for an opinion or a law.

It is quite clear, at least to me, that most of the students I have taught—and their parents—have no idea whatsoever what faith really means, despite the fact that nearly everything they claim to "know" and every opinion and decision they ever make is an act of faith.

Faith is Greg Louganis. When he climbed that ladder and leapt into the empty air, it was no blind leap in the dark. It was an opinion—a decision—based on all those uncountable other dives, on his consistently demonstrated skill, on the advice of his coach. Not a leap in the dark; a *calculated* risk, based on an enormous body of evidence which—still—was not conclusive enough to compel assent or guarantee a successful result.

Brain scientists claim that the two lobes of the brain have quite different functions (and since I'm no expert, I must take it on faith that they know what they're talking about and have no reason to deceive me). The left brain is analytical: it gathers data, sifts it, puts the best of it into logical sequence in order to draw a conclusion, and puts that conclusion out to be critiqued. The right brain is imaginative: it has hunches, sees a question in context, "senses" that this particular answer—even if the evidence is still inconclusive—"feels right." Thus, since the evidence available to solve any problem or arrive at any decision is rarely, if ever, "so clear and distinct that I have no occasion to doubt it," as Descartes demanded, a purely left-brain decision is impossible. Or at least half-witted.

The left brain is associated, unfortunately, with what we have always considered "masculine": decisiveness, rigid logic, impartiality. The right brain is associated with what we have wrongly dubbed "feminine": receptivity, creativity, and, alas, bias and feather-headed sentimentality.

---

66 *Most of the students I have taught—and their parents—have no idea whatsoever what faith really means.* 99

The left brain is "Greek": highly speculative; a statement is trustworthy (epistemologically sound) if it is logical and reasonable in itself and consistent with other already tested truths; it is "the scientific method." The right brain is "Hebrew": less speculative and more intuitive; a statement is trustworthy because the speaker has proven himself or herself to be worthy of trust.

The two travelers at Emmaus "knew" Jesus "in the breaking of the bread," a conviction neither capable of—nor, for the two men, needful of—logical proof. Yet their conclusion was, for all its lack of rigid logic, nonetheless rational. To take a homelier example: a lie detector is a far more scientific way of establishing whether a person is telling the truth, but I would put my money on the person's mother every time.

The left brain deals with knowledge, using definitions: the "head," as in "head trip." The right brain deals with understanding, insight, wisdom, using symbols: the "heart," as in "heartfelt." Hopkins captured Margaret's quite genuine awareness of human mortality: "Nor mouth heard, no nor mind, expressed / What heart heard of, ghost guessed."

The strict scientific method achieves its goals by rigorously excluding the subjective and unconfirmable right brain. But even the so-called "soft" sciences, like philosophy and theology and sociology, also seem resolutely to downplay the right brain as some kind of "weak sister," purposely rendering themselves psychologically tone-deaf and color-blind in order to cling to an unflinching objectivity.

Surely our utilitarian, Gradgrind education gives the right brain short shrift. In a budget crunch, the choice between cutting math and cutting art is not a choice at all. Even poetry is so much left-brain exam fodder; rarely are students required to write poems, just analyze them. The Scholastic Aptitude Tests, the narrow gate into higher education, are strictly a left-brain assessment of the candidate's left brain. And, to be realistic, how would one objectively assess a candidate's insight, understanding, savvy—without being biased by his or her own subjective opinions? And, again realistically, it is far easier for a teacher to photocopy and grade canned objective questions than to plough through Everests of ill-conceived, clumsily worded, all-over-the-lot essays.

And so the right brain—the avenue to understanding and wisdom and faith—atrophies, or it becomes bloated with junk food. If there is any reason for the popularity of rock music, romantic novels, comic books, and sex-and-violence films, it is starvation of the right brain.

Part of the distrust of the right brain is due simply to sloppy thinking and sloppy word choice. Right-brain hunches seem untrustworthy because they are somehow "emotional," because both hunches and emotions are called "feelings." But an emotion is a nonrational response to a stimulus; a hunch is a rational statement of what the speaker genuinely believes is the truth. If someone reading *Playboy* feels a rush of lust, that's a nonrational emotion; if someone says, "I have a feeling she's the girl I'm going to marry," that's a rational statement. Not a logical statement, but nonetheless a rational one.

But the downplay of the right brain's function in human knowledge is not merely the result of scientific condescension to anything less than objectively verifiable fact (except perhaps for the lamentable case of Carl Sagan). Each of us, no matter what our scientific background, lives in an age of pervasive low-grade paranoia. "Everybody's got an angle; they're all out to get you; keep your guard up." Especially in the area of religious faith, we want certitude before committing ourselves, simply because we've been hoodwinked so often before: Santa Claus was a hoax; masturbation doesn't in fact give you warts on the palms; and, in that awful betrayal at the kindergarten doorway, even my beautiful and loving mommy metamorphosed into the wicked stepmother right before my eyes, stranding me among those strangers. More importantly, accepting a religion is not the same as choosing a political party; I'm accepting fealty to a God I can neither see nor touch; I am submitting myself to a moral code based on a *God's* control of the natures and purposes of things and people and not my own. If I'm betting my life and all its choices on this decision, I'm not going off that high board until I have incontestable "scientific" proof.

The laughable trouble with that insistence is that such certitude is utterly impossible, even to a scientist dealing with science. Most people who make that demand for incontestable proof know very little about real science. Their only direct experience with it has been the "cookbook" science of high school and college, where the scientific "experiments" are not experiments at all but rather recipes guaranteed to have predictable results as long as the student doesn't make a mistake. When a real scientist goes into her laboratory at Sloan-Kettering, she doesn't expect to find the cure for cancer within an hour period—or this semester—or even in her whole career. She is approaching the truth, hemming it in more closely but never fully grasping it, which is all we can do with any research. There will always be more to discover about any truth.

---

66 *If there is any reason for the popularity of rock music . . . and sex-and-violence films, it is starvation of the right brain.* 99

Despite the fact that Werner Heisenberg won the Nobel prize over half a century ago for announcing the principle of uncertainty, those who naively wait for "scientific proof" don't realize that even scientists do not expect anything better than a "high degree of probability." Real scientists very wisely couch their findings not in absolute dogmatic formulas but in hypotheses: these conclusions are not carved in stone; there is still more to be discovered; but this is a conclusion closer to the truth than we were before.

What makes the demand for "scientific proof" before commitment to religious faith even more comical is that the very people who demand it put their lives daily into the hands of doctors, pilots, and cooks—without the slightest evidence of their competence, without even thinking to ask questions about it. In every medical school, some doctor surely had to have graduated last.

What's more, any real scientist knows that every scientific breakthrough began in the right brain, not in

the left. Newton and Einstein and Salk began with a
hunch, then sat down to establish logically whether their
hunch was right or not. The same could be said of the
generals and revolutionaries and entrepreneurs who
change the direction of human history, whom the man
or woman in the street pictures as coldly calculating,
purely "masculine" geniuses. They are, indeed, but only
because they put their analytical acuity at the service
of a dream, only because of the "marriage" of their
"masculine" and "feminine" intelligences. Michelangelo
had a soaring imagination, but he was also a most
meticulous draftsman; Mme. Curie was a painstaking
woman of intellect, but one who also "saw" a single vial
of radium lurking somewhere in a black hillock of
pitchblende.

Reality eludes the cookie-cutter categories and
definitions of the left brain seeking answers on its own.
My dictionary takes forty-three lines to define "love," and
still leaves me wondering. On the other hand, a little
muddy kid in a doorway holding out a bunch of droopy
dandelions says "love," too, and says it better, more
satisfyingly than the forty-three lines of my dictionary.

An act of faith is an opinion, a belief. The old cliché is
false: seeing is not believing; seeing is knowing. I don't
believe that the walls of my room are white; I know it.
But I don't *know* that God exists—or is benevolent and
not sadistic, or was enfleshed in Jesus Christ—or that I
will survive death. I believe all those things. I have a great
deal of evidence to support my beliefs, but I could be
wrong. There have been many geniuses who believed in
God, but there have been many who didn't.

The crucial question in studying the act of faith is—
logically, at least—peripheral to it: how many people
actually make an act of faith in God—a calculated
commitment based on intensive left-brain research, and
an inward, right-brain communion with the Object of the
quest, and a personal "sense" that their belief has a higher
degree of probability than its alternative? It is my "hunch"

that most people—especially but not exclusively the young—have made an act of faith based on their parents' act of faith, or on the evidence that "everybody believes in God," or on the fact that "you've got to believe in something." But few give me the "feeling" they've reasoned out their opinion and based it not only on reason but on actual experience of God. Perhaps that is at the root of so many answering "true" to "Faith is a blind leap in the dark."

The act of faith is an opinion, an opinion about what human beings are for, an opinion about what will make the one life I have worth living—and what will not. It is, in fact, the philosophy of life on which I base *all* other opinions and choices, *the* touchstone by which I judge their validity. But an opinion is only as good as the evidence that backs it up.

Most believers who have been educated above the level of unquestioning ingestion of the catechism have at least some left-brain basis for their belief. If sales of religious books are an indicator, a sizable number continue to accumulate new evidence and insights, though one would hardly expect Hans Kung's Christian readership to equal *TV Guide*'s Christian readership, and much of the body of religious literature that is read is hardly adult. The Letters to the Editor sections of most diocesan newspapers seem to give painful evidence that a large number at least of those with the courage to write letters have not raised their adult understanding of their faith from the Baltimore Catechism (which was written for children) and from literalist images of God which were the only ones available to writers twenty centuries ago.

What's more, what I said above about education in general was and is as true of religious education: almost exclusively left-brain, and, at least for those trained before Vatican II had worked its way down, not only left-brain but unquestioning because unquestionable. Seminary training in philosophy and theology was from manuals which, in many cases, were little more than more complex versions of the catechism, and those trainees came out to teach in universities.

Even methods of prayer were heavily left-brain. Some methods, it is true, stressed using the imagination to place oneself "into" a biblical scene, but—at least in my own case—that was only so that I could pick up some trenchant insight I could write in my "light book" to prove to myself that I was making "progress" and not wasting time. If I can judge from the youngsters and adults with whom I work, their idea of praying is, on the one hand, "saying prayers" and, on the other hand, asking God to make a change in plans or give definitive left-brain answers to confusing problems. When people come up empty-handed too many times, so much for praying. Nobody seems to have told them God is saying, "Look, I'll try to give you some 'answers,' but I can't until you stop doing all the talking."

❝ The act of faith is an opinion, an opinion about what human beings are for. ❞

There was and is very little attempt to show adult and young Catholics how to short-circuit the analytical left brain entirely, to let go of being "in charge" of the exchange, to become vulnerable to God—if you will, "feminine" to God—not passive but *receptive*. Eastern methods of praying do that, but it is very difficult to find a left-brain, "cost-effective" way to justify the expenditure of time and discipline and patience needed for such a way of contacting God to "pay off."

But if it began early enough, when children are not only more malleable but less embarrassed by their imaginations, it could have a profound effect on the future of the Church. Children don't have to be taught to "let go of being in charge," because they're not. Let religious education teachers show them methods of relaxing, centering themselves, making an empty space and just letting God come in and rest awhile. (I cringed when I typed that. I could just *hear* some teachers saying, "But how will I grade them?")

In a very real sense, one's *image* of God—the picture we get in our minds when we hear that word—is far more important than one's left-brain *idea* of God. If a person's imagining of God is locked into the images of church art—the stone-faced dignity on a lofty throne or Jesus as a tubercular, blue-eyed goy—his or her dealings with God and insights into God, self, and the relationship between the two will be tragically constricted.

But need we limit our images of God to the images available to men and women two thousand years ago? One of the richest—and perhaps most unlikely—sources of insight into God for me in my own praying and for my attempts to make God less distant from the people I teach comes from science and science fiction. Understanding God and understanding modern science require exactly the same skill: imagination. The person who can become immersed in science fiction sees that reality is most certainly bigger, more varied, more fascinating than we suspect. "There are more things in heaven and earth, Horatio, than are dreamt of in your [left-brain] philosophy."

And reading some popularized higher science shows not only that science and religion are not antagonistic, but that the scientist is now climbing the same reality as the theologian—and with the same imaginative tools. To hear a hard-nosed physicist explaining the relationships of muons and gluons and quarks makes a theologian explaining the relationships of the Father and Son and Spirit sound less like the ravings of some desert shaman.

Scientists speak unabashedly about neutrinos—which have no discernible mass, no electrical charge, and go through the whole earth scarcely slowed down by the effort. If neutrinos had intelligence (and how would we determine they did not?), they'd have all the properties a less sophisticated audience gave to angels. Scientists are now seriously considering the possibility that when the last particle is cracked open, the ultimate "stuff" of the universe would be nonextended energy. Like God, "I am who am," the pool of existence out of which all things draw their existence. Scientists say there can be no entity which surpasses the speed of light, but that seems to me merely left-brain snobbery, and scientists delight in playing "What If?" What if there *were* an entity faster than light (and how would our limited metallic machines capture such a presence)? It would be so fast that it would be everywhere at once, so hyper-alive that it would be at rest. Like God.

God antedated time and space. It is inescapable, then, that God cannot age, that God has no genitals and is therefore neither male nor female. But my problem is that I *am* in time and space, and both lobes of my brain are time-space oriented. My right-brain symbols—just as my left-brain definitions—deal with entities that are real but intangible, like love and atoms and God. They are all hypothetical, less than completely adequate. But I want to keep improving them, to cut down a bit more my distance from the truth. I find, personally, that praying to "a Person made of light," who lurks beneath and leaks out from everything I see, immeasurably more helpful than an old personage on a throne.

Jesus said that unless we become as little children, we cannot even discover the Kingdom, much less enter it. What do children have that all of us have lost? Wonder, exuberance, trust, a tireless addiction to asking "Why?" and, at the root of them all, an imagination uncontaminated by analysis, counting-the-cost, progress, and fear of others' expectations. Their imaginations objectify

their fears in monsters in the closet; they are young
enough and humble enough to see elves crouched in
cowslips and sense God shining out all over the place.

66 *One's image of God . . . is far more
important than one's left-brain idea
of God.* **99**

It is not merely imagination we need; it is also
humility—vulnerability before the truth: God is greater
than our minds' ability to capture God, to net God in our
definitions and symbols. As Chesterton says, the wise man
or woman does not try to cross the infinite sea—thus
taming it, making it finite. Instead, they float on it,
blissfully.

With our calculating left brains, we can know a great
deal *about* God. But it is only with our right brains—
vulnerable, receptive, "feminine"—that we will ever know
God.

FIVE

Converting the Baptized

At the end of the first act of *The Skin of Our Teeth,* when the Ice Age has shouldered the Montreal Cathedral as far south as Saint Alban's, Vermont, and it's so cold the dogs are sticking to the sidewalks, George and Maggie Antrobus are trying to jam facts into the heads of their children, Gladys and Henry, just in case they survive, random bits like: "Six times nine are fifty-four," and "In the beginning, God created the heavens and the earth . . ."

I sometimes wonder if we might be doing the same, each of us in our own soundproofed phone booths: throwing out anything and everything, just in case something might stick. Or as if we're training children for careers playing Trivial Pursuit.

Every year, I ask seniors: "You've endured this education schtick for the last eleven years; did you ever ask *why?* Once you're seventeen, it's not the law anymore. 'Well, everybody sez ya gotta get a education.' Well, four hundred years ago, everybody used to say the earth was flat, but they were wrong. If your only purpose is strictly utilitarian (i.e., to get a better job), then there's almost no connection whatever between what you take in class and what you'll be doing the rest of your lives. You don't need calculus to balance a checkbook, and you don't need irregular French verbs to run a lucrative French restaurant. All you need is guts, hard work, and the shrewdness to capitalize on your breaks. Frank Sinatra dropped out in ninth grade, Peter Jennings when he was seventeen; Hitler never even got into art school; Einstein and Barbara Tuchman never got Ph.D.'s. And each, in his or her chosen field, did reasonably well. The smart thing to do is ask your parents for the forty grand to set you up in business.

"For at least eleven years, you do something 150 days a year, for no other reason than 'everybody says.' And you never once asked *why* 'everybody says.' And in all these eleven years, I bet nobody's asked you even to think about it till now. Isn't that funny?"

Actually, they don't think it's funny at all. Because it's true. In eleven years of education, nobody ever told them why they do it. "Where ya goin'?" "Don't ask me, ask my hoooorse!"

But I wonder if that isn't actually true of us, too. We all obviously decided to be teachers. Accepting the job of parent is, *ipso facto,* accepting the job of teacher. Others of us, for reasons more prodigal than prudent, decided to be professionals at it. For very laudable and self-sacrificing and no doubt quite vague motives, we chose to make our meager living helping kids to learn, to open their lives, to share what we'd learned ourselves. But the gauzy pink honeymoon doesn't last. We settle into a routine; we cope with balkiness in the kids, and attendance slips, and detention, and the mindless proctoring and 'cause-we-have-to department meetings. And, before long, the impossible dream sags into a job, and Don Quixote and Aldonza are glad enough to abandon the windmills at three o'clock and head home to a couple of iced martinis and "Family Feud." A cynical caricature, but not without its vaguely unsettling truth.

Thus, I would like to try bringing down two horses of a different color with the same stone—or to be more precise, not to say honest—five stones. I'd like, first, to consider five ways in which, even if we can't assure the Christian conversion of our young, we can at least lessen their resistance to it when God enters their lives (which is inevitable). And also to show how teachers who are not in religious education or counseling—even non-Catholic or non-Christian teachers, and parents—no matter how long ago their last brush with Christian learning, can be a genuine part of the apostolic venture, without even once mentioning the name Jesus.

Perhaps our students won't waken to the gospel—or even to the need for a personally validated philosophy or myth or ethic—while we still have them in our schools and homes. But grace builds on nature; you can't sow seed on ground unplowed and unprepared for it. If our students graduate with terminal senioritis, if they aren't curious, humble before the truth, if they don't know how to think clearly, if they don't care even about one another after four years, if they aren't even courageous enough to raise their hands in class, there's little hope they'll even be able to comprehend the gospel—much less heed its call to become prophets, apostles, and healers.

My patron saint as a teacher is Annie Sullivan. How many hours and days did she draw apparently silly signs in Helen Keller's uncomprehending hands? But she trusted. She knew that, one day, Helen would bump into that pump—or into something—and suddenly would come the thunderous realization: I'm not alone!

"Paul plants; Apollos waters; God makes it grow." Parents and teachers can't convert the young—just help clear the road.

These are the five things I believe *all* teachers and parents not only can do but *must* do—not only alone in the soundproofed phone booths but knowingly, actively in concert with one another—no matter what the year, no matter what the department.

1. Make students genuinely aware and curious.
2. Teach them to be humble and honest before the data.
3. Teach them how to think—logically, thoroughly, open-mindedly, accurately.
4. Teach them to care about one another.
5. Teach them to stand up and be counted.

Maybe if we do "only" that, we might not yet be Christian schools or families, but we're heading in the right direction.

---

66 *Parents and teachers can't convert the young—just help clear the road.* **99**

---

1. Make Students Genuinely Aware and Curious

Students have to know, right from the first day, in terms *they* understand and value, *why* any sane person should expend time and effort—not to mention money—to ingest this data. When does it pay off—and not five years down the road or on the Great Come and Get It Day? "And don't tell me, 'It's on the syllabus,' or 'Everybody has to take it.' If you can't tell me that, in terms I can appreciate—if you don't even know yourself why I should do it—then I'll endure it, but I won't take it."

I had an unfortunately pyrotechnic encounter with a fellow curmudgeon last year. I had discovered that day that I'd be graced to teach an entire *year* of "The Church and Catholic Thinkers"—to high school juniors. Now, I can't think of many topics less calculated to arouse any student still in the mesmerizing fog of puberty than that baby. So, I asked, "How do I get them even to care about the Church? If I don't, it's a year of treading water." And this old veteran said, "Just teach the syllabus. And every once in a while you go in and wave the flag around." How ardently my soul burned to sit in on one of his classes!

Education begins in wonder, or it doesn't begin. Anything I was ever force-fed was just so much imminent garbage. We all know that's true, but too often we forget. The majority of the kids I teach whose grades are hovering in the 70s and/or who are wallowing in the cesspool of senioritis tell me the reason they don't learn is that they're lazy. Not at all. If I told them the Playgirl of the Month was parading around the gym in the very attire or lack thereof that won her fleeting fame, my hunch is they could overcome their inertia and amble on down there. Nobody is lazy, just unmotivated.

We don't have to be "Sesame Street." But we all have to spend at least as much time on how we hook and hold the students' interest as on what we have to say. At the very least, we ourselves ought to know *why* any future physician should read *Hamlet* and why any prospective lawyer should factor quadratic equations and why any aspiring CEO should memorize *amo, amas, amat.*

At least by junior year, we've got to start battering down the walls between departments, to show students not only that each of our disciplines is studying the same data under a different kind of microscope, but also that each of us is still interested in the insights of the other departments and can enrich our own discipline with them. At a school I used to serve, several of us wanted to have a senior elective called "Effing the Ineffable," trying to show that physics and religion and sociology were all trying to capture in words and pictures and diagrams— each time a touch less inadequately—realities that none of us could see. But the office said it would be a nightmare to schedule, so, year after year, it was stillborn and we stopped trying. Lorenzo Reed, a Jesuit administrator for many years, once gave a dictum administrators should tattoo on their palms: "Anything educationally desirable is administratively feasible."

If science seems hostile to religion, if our students don't realize that we see only the slightest bit of what's there, if they don't accept the fact that "there are more things in heaven and earth, Horatio, than are dreamt of in your philosophy"—or your science or religion, Christianity doesn't have a chance.

2. Teach Students to Be Humble and Honest before the Data

Each of us has heard this from students, no matter what our discipline: "Do you want what we really think or *your* interp'atation?" One time with a group of juniors, I was doing a poem by Amy Lowell, called "Wind and Silver." It's a simple poem:

> *Greatly shining,*
> *The Autumn moon floats in the thin sky,*
> *And the fishponds shake their backs*
> *And flash their dragon scales*
> *As she passes over them.*

Nothing simpler. Just a picture of a pond, and the moon makes the ripples look like dragon scales. Hand up. "I've got a different interpretation." Okay, as long as the data support it; a poem's not a Rorschach test. "I think it's about a U-2 flight over Red China." Momentary readjustment of mandible. Where's the evidence? "Right there! 'Dragon scales.'" You've taken two words and spun out your own poem! "That's *your* opinion." I tried sarcasm: Why couldn't it be a U-2 flight over medieval England; they had dragons. "That's *your* opinion." Then I had him: Look at the end of the poem—Amy Lowell, 1874–

1925. She was *dead!* There *was* no Red China! There *were* no U-2s! And he said . . . "That's *your* opinion." The last thing I recall before they arrived with the straitjacket was several stout football players prying my thumbs from his throat.

---

66 *Education begins in wonder, or it doesn't begin.* 99

We forget that kids are just emerging from near autism, where the only things real are what concerns them personally. It doesn't matter if she *is* a slut or not; what's important is what I *think* of her. If we don't challenge that, forcefully, meaningfully, in every department and at every family dinner, they're going to go on believing, "My opinion is as good as anybody else's." Nope. Your opinion is *only* as good as the evidence that backs it up. Your opinion on physics is *not* as good as Einstein's—or even as good as mine; your opinion on the first ten pages of a book are not as good as the Nobel prize committee's.

In *every* department, we have to teach epistemology.

I don't tell the tree what it is; it tells me. If I'm drunk and say, "My, what a big green ostrich! With no legs!" my opinion's worth diddly-poop. My opinion is only as good as the process that preceded it. If I see demi-*derriere*-edly, categorize demi-*derriere*-edly, judge demi-*derriere*-edly, and I have a demi-*derriere*-ed vocabulary, what's my opinion gonna be? You got it.

Thus, I don't tell atoms—or a fetus, or human sexuality, or God—what they are; they tell me. If "everybody's opinion's as good as anybody else's," Christianity doesn't have a chance.

3. Teach Students How to Think

Most kids I've taught believe they know how to think. They don't. They know how to mull; they know how to worry an idea; they know how to grab hold of a few words in the question and BS about it—fill space with words for as long as you give them—but they don't know how to think. They don't know how to *reason.* And a great deal of that is our fault. We get locked into our own disciplines and syllabi and forget that we're all teaching—or should be teaching—precisely the same thing: how the mind works.

Sad to say, most of the data we so painstakingly prepare and teach and test students will not only never use but never remember. The formulas and dates and processes and personalities are already slipping into oblivion before they even finish the final. The data are not the point; the data are like the paper Xerox uses to test out its machines. The data and paper are unimportant, garbage; the important thing is what processing them does to the machine.

Thinking is a relatively simple process—to describe:

1. gather the data,
2. sift the data to get the best,
3. put the data into some kind of logical sequence so that you can
4. draw a conclusion, and
5. put that conclusion out to be critiqued.

That is—quite simply—the scientific method, and it should be applied as unyieldingly in theology as in chemistry. Which of us doesn't do that? What do we do in labs? What do we do when we ask kids to write essays—gather, sift, outline, conclude, and allow me to critique. That's the way the mind *works.* That's the way we come to understand things. It's the whole purpose of basic education. And it's the one thing we never tell the kids.

That's what we're all trying to teach, in every department. The data is only fodder. We want kids to learn how to think—logically, thoroughly, open-mindedly, accurately. If we could only make that our *common* goal, we'd have a chance.

Every time any one of us lets a copied lab slip by without sitting down with the kid and talking about it, every time we take what is obviously a ten-minute essay filled with swamp gas and dignify it with even a 70, every time we fail to hold a kid for downs for logic and evidence, we *are* the enemy.

We *must,* at the very least, teach students how to think. All the dogmas and certitudes we pump into them today will be laughable tomorrow. Did the people who taught us in high school envision the Baby M case, or genetic engineering, or wholesale abortion, or nuclear waste? The problems our kids will face haven't even been invented yet. The *only* thing we can give them—in every discipline—is the skills to think, honestly.

If we don't teach them how to think, Christianity hasn't got a chance against the propaganda.

4. Teach Students to Care About One Another

Like our families, our schools are often worn down by the day-to-day crap, confronting original sin in all its infinite forms, to the point where we'll settle for civility and politeness—basic unruffled discipline—rather than find ways to break down kids' self-protective barriers, strip away the shyness, let them see that, behind all the macho and prom-queen masks, we all fear the same things and we all want the same things: to love and be loved. Not just on retreats, in school.

All our gush about "The Alexander VI High *family*" and the "Savanarola Academy *community*" strikes me—in face of the evidence—as almost pure bullroar. We are no more a community than a congregation of strangers on a bus. Year after year, I ask seniors to look around the room and count the faces they can't put a name to, how many they've never spent ten minutes with or eaten lunch with. Enlightening. Most of the friends they do have they met by accident—same part of the alphabet, same team, same penchant for detention, same time to hide out in the library from the novice sadists. But after the laudable but short-lived orientation days in first year, do we do anything to go beyond the accidental acquaintances that arise—at least for the ones with the courage to go out for an activity?

❝ The scientific method . . . should be applied as unyieldingly in theology as in chemistry. ❞

I stumbled on one such way in my junior Church class. We were studying the difference between a congregation and a community, and I asked them what kept *us* from being a community, what divided us: the shyness, the one-upmanship, the cliques. So I handed out a class list and had the students check off the ones they really didn't know. Since then, once a week, when we're brainstorming for the weekly essay, I pair them up with somebody they've checked off, and they brainstorm together. It's a small thing, but perhaps I'm heading in the right direction.

If we could make young people truly care about one another, we'd have to worry less about stealing. We'd have fewer fights. We'd hear less of "guido" and "nerd" and "dweeb" and "faggot." We'd be doing our jobs. Unless we can get them to know one another, we can't hope they'll care for one another. And if we can't make them care for one another—just as good kids, after four full years—Christianity hasn't got a chance.

5. Teach Students to Stand Up and Be Counted

Martin Luther King said anyone who had nothing worth dying for didn't deserve to live. But if the vast majority of our kids don't have the courage—or the interest—even to put up their hands in class (a relatively unintimidating forum), I doubt they're too promising candidates for Christian prophets, apostles, and healers—not to mention voting, or writing a letter to an editor, or devoting their lives to public service, or running for political office, or winning the Nobel Peace Prize. Oh, we talk at them about those things, but do we ever *show* them they can make a difference?

For over twenty years, I've asked seniors what they would do about a truly ineffective teacher. Typical response: gripe to friends, doodle, write letters, get it on my own. Some few went to the principal or the chair, but "nothing happened," so they joined the doodlers. And the teacher went on, year after year, labotomizing more students and failing at his or her life work. Worse, those students graduated believing "nobody can change anything."

Teachers and parents could surely give our young the lesson of the importunate widow: you don't gripe just once; you go back again. And again. And, if you're smart, you don't go alone. They can also praise that persistence. "I don't want you merely to be a material success. I want you to *change* things. I don't want you to be goddamn sheep—because God does damn human beings who cringe like sheep before things that *can* be changed."

You learn confidence first with small things: the unfair teacher, the cafeteria prices, the doors in the school john off the hinges for years. Would the school dare have small town meetings to encourage kids to speak out, tactfully, without fear of reprisal? Too much hassle? Too risky? If we can't get them even to do that, Christianity doesn't have much of a chance.

Before we can make young people even comprehend what Christianity asks, we have to humanize them. What makes humans different from animals—or from savages—is that we can know and love. If we make them curious, humble, able to think honestly, loving, confident, then Christianity has a chance. If we can't do that, we'd all be better off—and better paid—working in napalm factories.

SIX

In Praise of Doubt

Were the founder of Boys Town still alive, I assume he'd amend his famous dictum: "There's no such thing as a bad boy—or girl." To that I'd add O'M's Corollary: "There's no such thing as an irreligious boy or girl"— provided the listener (for the moment) understands the word *religious* not in any specified, denominational sense (Catholic, Protestant, Muslim, Buddhist), but rather as describing someone honestly and earnestly seeking a coherent worldview.

I base my claim on the unassailable evidence of cliché: there are no atheists at Fort Apache. And adolescence—no matter how pampered and blissful in the brochures—is precisely that: blitzkrieg from all sides, corners, overhead, and underground, by a nightmarish coalition of most contradictory allies—puberty, parents, peers, and potential dates; plus coaches, teachers, pastors, and college admissions officers; plus hitherto unknown and presently unwanted responsibilities, fiscal, filial, and vocational; not to mention the hellhound id and the hatchet-faced superego. And the suicidal assaults of the mirror.

In such a chaos, the response may not be quite, "How long, O Lord? How long!" It may be merely, "What the hell's goin' *on?* Can anybody make any *sense* out of all this crapola?" Albeit colloquial, that is a sincere plea for a coherent worldview, for at least some kind of transitional map that might, eventually, lead to the map we more conventionally know as formal religion.

I find confusion and doubt are not only very healthy but requisite for an adult faith. Doubt is a clear indication that one's previous certitudes are no longer capable of digesting and making sense of life, and—in the healthy individual—sends him or her in search of answers that will be, at least for the proximate future, better. It is precisely this prickly agnosticism that sent the young Chesterton off in search of his own personal heresy, which, when he put the final touches to it, turned out to be Orthodoxy. Thus, I find the fretting of adults over the religious skepticism of the young understandable, but unintelligible—especially from adults who tirelessly bemoan the loss of Chesterton as a religious role model.

Young people who do *not* go through this crisis of faith will either line up like mannequins and wear their "faith" like a Sunday hat, or they will pitch the whole thing into the Goodwill bag along with Santa Claus and the tooth fairy—and live lives just as surface and spiritless as the churchgoers they sneer at.

Dr. M. Scott Peck is right: "There is no such thing as a good hand-me-down religion." If it is to be more than mere lifelong lip service, religion must come only after a quest as harrowing as the quest for personal identity.

Internalized learning—even religious learning—must begin with genuine curiosity, or it will never begin at all. Authentic learning (as opposed to rote memorizing) is impossible unless the learners question what they are told, try to poke holes, sniff for rats, challenge the validity of all the shamans and all their shibboleths—till they can say, "This is not my parents' faith; this is mine."

However, most born-Christians are still taught that doubt and skepticism are temptations even more lethal than lust. Adult Christians do not want to seem wavering in their faith for two reasons: one, their honest doubts could be contagious, and two, honest doubt might force them back to reexamine convictions they thought were cast in bronze from their childhood.

❝ I find confusion and doubt are not only very healthy but requisite for an adult faith. ❞

Ironically, however, it is precisely adult Christians' unbending, seeming certitude and their vigilance against doubt that undermine their own credibility as authentic believers, on the one hand, and on the other inhibit young people's personal apprehension and ownership of religious values. We ask them to invest their lifelong trust in a system of beliefs and practices based on less skepticism (and therefore less personally convincing evidence) than we would focus on a used-car dealer.

Concerned Christian parents often believe the sole cause of their children's disinterest—or even disdain—for organized religion is that they are spoiled, that God has never brought them to their knees (which is, admittedly, a privileged place from which to see who God really is and who we really are). But this fear within good parents for their children's souls is itself an unconscious lack of faith: "If I can't make them face and accept God, they'll never find God," forgetting that God will find each individual when and where each is ready to be found. Cf. Paul, Augustine, Thomas Merton.

In our less fretful and more objective moments, we know that the ways of God—written into the nature of human life—will inexorably give the lie to that unconscious adolescent arrogance, in ways both tragic and trivial. Whether it be "Why did she turn me down for Friday night?" or "Why can't I make him love me as much as I love him?" or "Why did my child die?" there will be many, many times when confrontation with God is no longer avoidable. In the meetings between God and our children, we are merely matchmakers. And often *yentas*, at that.

The far more likely cause is lack of motivation, a personally felt reason *why* religion and religious practice should occupy our children's time and attention. This imperviousness will not be cured by thunderous threats. Achieving more than mere tolerance of religion is in a different league from achieving a tolerance of broccoli. We are asking a life commitment.

Theology is what we know about God; *belief* is what we personally accept of what we know; *religion* is what we do about what we believe. It is liberating to accept the painful truth: we can offer only theology to our young; belief and religious practice are free choices only they can make for themselves.

Theology

Theology is beyond the scope of this essay, but I would hazard the opinion that our present catechetical content is too much, too soon. Children are force-fed answers to questions that will not become meaningful for another ten years, if ever. And when the problems actually arise, the answers will be remembered, if at all, as "kids' stuff." Our students come to believe that all the ill-digested religious doctrines carry the same weight—and penalty—(because they did on the test) whether the doctrine concern masturbation or Mass, abstinence during Lent or the divinity of Jesus.

Is there a reason why children should be burdened with the threeness of God in any more than a cursory way? Is there a reason why, although we would not lay the undiluted *Lear* on high school students, we can and must lay the undiluted Luke on them? Is there a reason why, even in college and beyond, otherwise adult Christians equate—univocally—the Church with God, as if God were unfree to speak through any other channel, as if any "mistake" the Church might make deprives God of all credibility?

Belief

Belief is what one—freely—accepts of what he or she has been told or experienced. Of course, if the material has been incomprehensible, totally divorced from the youngsters' ability to grasp it as personally meaningful, it will not linger long in their minds after the exam. The test of religious learning's relevance, I think, is whether children sense its genuine importance to their parents—not merely as demonstrated in their children's grades or religious conformity, but as a body of life-giving ideas so integral to human fulfillment that the parents themselves continue to probe them—long after some "system" stops requiring that they do. If religious belief is quite obviously peripheral to their parents' lives (compared, say, to educational, athletic, and social achievement), why would the children consider religious belief focal to their own lives?

Before he died, Dan Lord, S.J., who spent a lifetime tirelessly evangelizing youth in sodalities and summer schools of Catholic Action, wondered aloud to a friend whether, after all that, he might have done better working with the children's parents. Which might give educators and pastors pause. If parents could respond to their children's doubts, with a confidence energized by consistent probing of their own religious beliefs, as adults, and with an honest vulnerability that precluded the need to dominate the argument, at home where doubts arise more naturally than in an intimidating classroom, adult to becoming-adult—then the youngsters might find a belief based not on blind surrender of intellect and will, but on a loving, honest sharing of the search for God which never ends.

❝ God will find each individual when and where each is ready to be found. ❞

Religion

Religious practice has always been a somewhat unreliable touchstone of religious belief. Students call to witness pantheons of family friends who never go to church but out-saint Maria Goretti, along with crusty pillars of the church who could abash Fagin—staunchly denying that reciprocal cases could also be possible. But their skepticism is not total simplism. If they are asked to attend church at least on Sundays—not merely when they are with parents, but when they are alone and free—they need a reason more internally suasive than "because I say so," or "because the Church says so." Not a guarantee of effectiveness, but at least a motivation meaningful to them. Parents have often proved objectively wrong about blacks or Jews or welfare; the Church was objectively wrong about Galileo and slavery and usury. We are asking for a life commitment, long after we are gone, and after they have cars of their own for Friday night and are demonstrably distant from Skid Row.

The most frequent objection I've heard in twenty years of teaching religious education is: "I believe in God. Why do I have to go to Mass? Can't I just talk to God in

the woods?" to which I offer a brace of abrasive answers:
"Of course, but why does it have to be either/or?" and
more importantly, "When was the last time you actually
did it?"

My responses, of course, as with the brief discussion
of theology above, do not cope with the liturgy itself which
is, to very many young people, personally unmeaningful,
boring, and irrelevant. But to tell them that they really
should like it is as effective as telling them castor oil is
good for them.

The one motive I have found young people susceptible
to is gratitude. If the one who gave me life asks, "Do *this*
in memory of me," I do it.

As a support of that motivation, the psychiatrist Erik
Erikson suggests that the practice of formal religion, at
the very least, serves to promote a healthy personality—
offering at regular intervals, on the one hand, a sense of
trust in oneself and in a supportive community, while on
the other hand giving visible admission to the existence
of evil, in oneself and in the world around us.

All religions have in common a periodic, childlike
surrender to a Provider—formally acknowledging one is
not "in charge" of life, and yet also that one is not alone
in life either. There is God; there are the others. Religious
practice demonstrates, publicly, one's smallness and
dependence. It admits, in song and in prayer, one's frailty,
misdeeds, misthoughts, unhealthy intentions. It confesses
an inner division we *all* feel and appeals for divine
encouragement to achieve some greater, more honest
inner wholeness. It challenges the self to a larger life than
one may have planned on living.

What's more, religious practice is an acknowledgment
that trust in oneself is not enough; one needs to trust and
be trusted by others. The restoration of the individual to
wholeness must also be reflected in the growing sense of
wholeness in the community. To be sure, that "sense of
belonging" can come from some nonreligious group: the

Elks, the Campfire Girls, the army, the team. But such belonging has only a horizontal, this-world dimension. Those extensions of the isolated self are, of course, far richer than confinement to the limits of one's own skin, one's own family, one's own small clique. But it is not a union enlivened by the sense of the *numinous* dimension of full human life—that is, the dimension of the human spirit, the part of our whole selves which feels awe at the grandeur of humanity and creation, which feels the need for honor, duty, loyalty, which tries to capture the elusive mystery of life in art, which yearns to penetrate the barriers that divide and categorize, and find a unity to our living.

In short, regular religious practice is an honest confrontation with who we really are.

That, of course, is the ideal. The actual embodiments of that ideal in a real liturgical situation very often fall far short of capturing it. But one of the reasons for that deadness lies outside the liturgical setting: the rest of the week. If one expects to experience the truly numinous only in one dutiful hour, once a week, he or she might as easily find true love in one hour, once a week, in a brothel. If there's been no time during the rest of the week to reflect, to feel awe, to sense a greater dimension to our living than the mere practical, there's little hope that one can walk into a church or synagogue, sit down, and get zapped.

Perhaps young people's true hunger for the numinous is a reason drugs have become such a popular, ersatz substitute. One gets the sense one might have had of the genuinely numinous, but without the carryover when the high has ended. The reason is that all that one has sacrificed for the high is not his or her defenses against vulnerability; all one has sacrificed is money. And what has been stimulated is not the human soul but only human nerves, as when one laughs when tickled—even though there's nothing really funny about it. Expecting the exhilaration of contact with the numinous without a genuine investment of self is like expecting welfare for the soul. The door into—and out of—oneself has only one handle, and it is on the inside. Neither the greatest liturgical minister nor the most supportive religious congregation can batter open that door. Not even God can.

> 66 *Regular religious practice is an honest confrontation with who we really are.* 99

The yearning of the young for the numinous is undeniable; it is, after all, what they were born for. We claim that the numinous fulfillment of human beings is achieved more fully in religious belief and practice than in any other human commitment. If their skeptical responses to our claims make us uneasy, anguished, fretful, that too is very healthy—indeed, a grace from God—impelling us back to rethink our own certitudes and the terms and symbols in which we encapsulate them. But only if we ourselves accept the grace to doubt.

SEVEN

Teenage Spirituality

Occasionally, people ask me questions as if I'd suddenly become the Carl Sagan of the teen universe. I grant that twenty-two years of reading about forty reflection papers each from what now amounts to about 3,500 high school and college students have given me perhaps a better insight into what teenagers think than, say, a first-time parent—and surely better than the teenager, but I still have more than a few reminders of my finitude and fallibility. One of them arrived in the mail one Friday, from a group of high school principals, asking me to give a workshop on teenage spirituality the next year in Tucson.

My first reaction was, of course, selfish: who wouldn't trade slush for sunshine in March? My second reaction was cynical, the result of trying to teach distributive justice too long to kids whose orthodontia payments alone would gobble up a yearful of welfare checks. That voice from the unredeemed part of me snorted, "Teenage spirituality is an oxymoron." By far the majority of the young men and women I've taught and teach—judging

by their responses to those 140,000 reflection papers—
have far less genuine spirituality than an aborigine
placating the gods in the Australian outback. For them,
the content of the word *spirit* is the same as in "a spirited
pony" or "school spirit"; it has far more to do with aspects
of "personality" than of "character."

But then the small voice of the redeemed part of me
whispered, "Pst! You don't even know what *spirituality*
means, do you?" And, as usual, that voice was spang on.
I'd used the word all my life, read books about it, heard
lectures about it. I'd written four books about praying.
And I didn't honestly know what the word meant. I
wonder if many people who use it just as commonly do
either. Far more importantly, we religious educators
spend a great deal of time trying to fill youngsters' minds,
to help them know more *about* God, but we spend
precious little trying to ignite their spirits, to help them
know *God,* person-to-Person, by themselves, without us.
So I figured I'd better sit down and teach myself a lesson,
which perhaps might be helpful to someone else.

Spirituality

My spirit is my soul—my self, my character, my who-
I-am. It's that potential within me that responds to the
numinous and the sacred in nature, in art, in people, in
God, that is humbled when it senses how the world is
charged with God's grandeur. It's where all the nebulous
and unquantifiable aspects of my self reside: honor, awe,
genuine sentiment, loyalty, remorse, patriotism, faith,
hope, love (when it's purged of self). Just as my hunger
for food is in my belly, and my hunger for reasons is in
my brain, my hunger to survive death lives in my soul.
But the state of my soul-life—my spirituality—is
something I can comprehend only vaguely, in a glass
darkly, as elusive as the moments that quicken it.

All the scholastic philosophers to the contrary
notwithstanding, human beings are quite definitely not

"rational animals." If that were the limit of our being, we would be merely apes with computers implanted—which is merely a variant of scientism. It is precisely that simplism C. S. Lewis lashes in *The Abolition of Man:* that unquestioned rationalist and materialist supposition that underlies most of our educational decisions, even in Christian schools: *"Mens sana in corpore sano."* Nope. If all we train are healthy minds in healthy bodies, we will get what Lewis calls "men without chests": alternately cerebral and visceral, but not human—because we've left out what makes us human: not the visceral, surely, nor even the cerebral, but the spiritual. It is the heart, not the brain (which we share with beasts), that makes us human—and not "heart" in the sense of the sentimental-ist, but heart in the sense Hopkins used for Margaret's sudden understanding of death:

> *Nor mouth had, no nor mind, expressed*
> *What heart heard of, ghost guessed.*

Neither belly nor brain can account for the "hope against hope" of surviving death.

Lewis's colleague, Dorothy Sayers, explains as well as anyone I've read both the Trinity and the human soul. In the triadic union of the godhead, the Father expresses himself—his Word—and in that very expression a power of loving is generated, who is the Spirit. Just so, in the fusion of mind and body, a third power is—or can be—generated: the human spirit.

The reductionists—among whom are most of our students—constantly assert that humans are no more than higher level animals. Beasts can sense dangers even humans can't; dolphins and whales communicate at enormous distances; animal mothers show great "love" for their young, even to the point of self-sacrifice. What they fail to account for is the difference between knowledge and understanding, and between affection and love—perhaps because they have been educated only to know and not to understand, and because they have felt only loyalty and affection but never genuine love. An animal might sacrifice for its own, but we can sacrifice even for our enemies. The reductionists surely don't consider that no sow, snoozing in maternal bliss in a ringlet of piglets, has her dreams disturbed by the certainty that she will one day die.

The human spirit is further distanced from the animal, not by a smeary and gradual change but by a quantum leap, in the fact that animal nature is a command, and human nature is an invitation. No tiger refuses to be tigerish, and no lion refuses to be leonine, but the daily newspapers are glutted with evidence that human beings refuse to be human. They act, in fact, precisely like no more than higher level animals—only with the added advantage of the human brain, which raises animal shrewdness and savagery to a capacity for saturation bombings and extermination camps. What allows us to call such wretches "inhuman" is not their lack of a body or a mind but their lack of a soul.

---

66 *Animal nature is a command, and human nature is an invitation.* 99

The genetic instructions in the human body are what Albert Rosenfeld calls "a framework of opportunities." The tiger and lion follow their inner programming automatically, but the human male with big shoulders and strong legs is free to work on them to become a Big League fullback—or he's free to pass them by and take up the violin. Just so with the human spirit. A ghetto kid can turn his squalor into a Horatio Alger story, and an advantaged kid can turn his opportunity into a Jay MacInerny story—because humans are free, and freedom resides in the soul. And we are free to actualize our human potential. Or not.

Just as the hungers of the human belly can be palliated with junk food and the hungers of the human mind sated by the *National Enquirer* and *Sporting News,* the hunger of the human spirit can get an ersatz jag from pep rallies and Boy Scout oaths and pop music. Most students I teach quote U-2 and Springsteen as if they were T. S. Eliot and Holy Writ. But the result is the same with the soul as with the belly and brain: flab. It is why so many of our young—and not-so-young—seem dis-spirited.

The spirit, which is the result of conscious marriage of cerebral and visceral, is what Romans called *anima.* Feminine. That view fits the metaphors of the soul and Church as the Bride of Christ. Lewis believes, then, that the proper posture of the soul before God—whether in a male or female—is "feminine": not in any way passive, but receptive, fertile, vulnerable, creative. In that sense, God comes to each of our souls, in a daily annunciation, and asks, "Conceive my Son in you today."

In that sense, then, the process of civilization—of humanization—has been a process of feminizing the macho-savage side of what are only potential human beings. The Viking or knight is merely an Olympic-class butcher without the minstrel to give his slaughter a meaning, a context, to make his story not merely titillate the mind but stir the soul. And Christianity took one quantum leap further: its hero not only eschewed battle but conquered by his sheer impotence.

As I struggled this far, the unredeemed voice became positively smug: "See?" The possibility of accessing the teenage soul seemed a task to daunt Hercules. "Teenage spirituality? In the nineties? Flat-out contradiction."

And yet I sense a soul-life in our young, like the yearning for freedom in the fifth-generation slave. It's in the grain. Except perhaps for the autist and sociopath, it can't be excised from any human being. It's born in us: the itch for Eden.

The Obstacles in the Audience

The new age—since the assassinations and Vietnam and Watergate—has witnessed the death of "Wow!" None of us will be caught again with our hearts on our sleeves. In a class of thirty, only one or two will admit having been moved to tears by a film. Patriotism shriveled to paying taxes and perhaps voting. What leaves the young openmouthed today? A Trans Am, a beautiful body, a spectacular goal, an explosive rock concert—all external, all soul-substitutes. In order to feel awe, one has—by definition—to feel small in contrast to the stimulus: a mountain at dawn, a star-strewn sky, the beloved, God. But the permanent posture of most youngsters now is not vulnerability but constant defensiveness, not on their knees but with their dukes up.

One reflection paper asks the student for his or her heroes; more and more in recent years, half the students answer, "I don't think I have heroes." It makes sense. A pervasive skepticism began to infect the American spirit after the downfall of the Camelot–Flower Child crusade. No hero or heroine can last long with an army of investigative reporters dogging their Achilles' heels. The media smother us with emotional programming we all know is phony but nonetheless fall for. "Value" is strictly a left-brain commodity, a solid return for your investment.

Another class, about values, pictures a little girl with a fifty-dollar bill in one hand and a stuffed rabbit in the other: "If, by some impossible turn of events, you were forced to throw one of those three into a furnace, which would you throw?" In the one hundred or so times I've done it, some wag inevitably says the little girl. Once that's behind us, the majority say the rabbit. Why? You take the fifty bucks and buy another—ignoring, of course, the fact that the money is the girl's. Then, gradually, it begins to dawn on some that the child has very little sense of the value of money, but that the worn-out rabbit is her most precious possession. There are two kinds of value, one easily quantifiable by the left brain, the other not so easily boxed in but resonating in the sensitized soul. Nor is the exercise based on "some impossible turn of events." Forty years ago, people faced just that choice: to process millions of little girls in incinerators, like garbage. Those who agreed still had human minds and human bodies, but they had lost hold of their human souls.

Another reflection is also enlightening: "Given a choice between a job you detested which paid an obscenely high salary, or a job you truly loved but made you, your spouse, and family really have to struggle to make ends meet, which would you take?" I've kept a running log, and 85 percent would choose to be miserable with the high salary. Their reasons sound noble: they would rather be unhappy if it gave their families "a good life." Rarely do they consider that their family's happiness might be affected by their week-long misery. Despite the fact that we've previously gone through Erikson's stages of disequilibrium necessary for human growth, no student ever wrote that he or she would be willing to let the children struggle in order to develop spine; they would rather give their children comfort than character. No student ever wrote that he or she would choose a spouse who'd rather have them, fulfilled, than a pool in the backyard. There is only one meaning to "the good life," and it has nothing whatever to do with Plato and Aristotle, much less Jesus Christ.

Many adults fail to realize how much "image" domi-nates the lives of the young. Since the caves, youngsters at puberty have suddenly awakened to an awareness of their faces and physiques: "Mom, am I pretty? . . . Is my body wimpy?" But today, exploiting that concern is a multibillion-dollar industry. The self-doubtful voices within the child are now amplified and multiplied until their lives are totally surrounded by judgmental mirrors. There are a variety of responses to that pervasive incitement to self-doubt: "cool," conformity, projection, alienation, one-upmanship—among many others. But all of these reactions are based on a judgment about surfaces, about personality rather than character. What you seem to be is far more important than who-you-are; nothing succeeds like the appearance of success.

But if the discovery of one's soul depends on vulnerability, how can we convince youngsters of the crucial importance of laying hold of a self—much less the painful effort of going in quest of it, when they spend most of their time on the defensive?

---

66 Many adults fail to realize how much 'image' dominates the lives of the young. 99

Not only do the ads and media subvert the search for the soul, but our children's education—both in school and at home—is almost exclusively surface and pragmatic. Teachers and parents fall back on the only motivation for learning they can think of: not to discover a self, a character, a philosophy of life, but to get a good job. Since Sputnik, "everybody knows" math and science are the important subjects, even for an aspiring lawyer or artist. Even the so-called "soft" disciplines like English and history are primarily analytical, left-brain. The object of education is to "master" the data, not to be vulnerable to it and follow wherever the subject chooses to lead. When parents ask, "How ya doin' in school?" they don't often mean, "Is it exciting?" but "How are your grades?"

The possibility of teenage spirituality is looking less and less likely. And yet, like any missionary, one becomes hypersensitive to any flicker of interest, any hint that there might be hope. The Iroquois let me tag along on their treks; the Mandarins cock a reluctantly quizzical eye at my sextant and my clocks. If parents and teachers can establish credibility with this skeptical audience in nonreligious, spiritual areas, there's a chance we might see that squinted face that's saying, "Hey, wait a minute. I may be missing something. You listen to . . . God?"

Sensitizing the Soul

The first step is to acknowledge that our primary obligation as Christian parents and educators is *not* the SATs. One would be an idealistic fool to ignore them, but they are not the reason we charge tuition and hang crucifixes in our classrooms. We have a duty to our students' minds, but we have a more profound duty to their souls, to sensitize them, feminize them so that no youngster—especially no boy—needs apologize for having one. Our task as apostles to the young is to lead them, like our Father, to understand and express the self—not merely the "sometime spirit" that emerges by chance during a dutiful Mass or during one of the astonishing, numinous, Oh-my-God! moments, but the spirit that *is* the child's true self. But that will require a major conversion, in teachers and administrators, from our pervasively pragmatic and efficient mind-set.

There is a natural potential in every human person, even nonreligious persons, that responds to the numinous and sacred in nature and art. And if grace builds on nature, we can begin our movement toward the spirituality that deals with God by sensitizing children early to that more accessible and less intimidating union with the powerful and invisible forces all around them (which are, in fact, the aliveness of God).

In grade school, rather than instruct children about sin (of which they are not yet capable) or about the Virgin Birth and Trinity (which baffled even Aquinas), let us teach them, once a week at least, ways of relaxing and centering themselves, opening themselves to God. Very young children are far better candidates for meditative, receptive, "feminine" prayer than adults. They are less uptight, less defensive, more imaginative. According to

Jesus, they are already in the Kingdom. Teach them to feel it, enjoy it, revel in it, perhaps even remain in it.

Sometime in or after first grade, learning gradually ceases being an adventure and becomes a boring chore. My hunch is that we feel we've finally lured them into our lair, and it's time to get down to the serious and efficient business of those SATs. Of course children have to wrestle for basic skills, but even though learning might not always be fun, it ought always to be intriguing. As "Sesame Street" consistently proves, children learn far faster when their curiosity is piqued, when they are given not answers but problems and sent off in quest of their own answers. It is not as efficient as "ingest-and-regurge," but the God we are trying to sensitize them to is quite obviously not as efficient as we'd like, either.

Every year, I'm amazed how many bright seniors have never read Aesop's fables or Grimm's fairy tales. They've never lived with dragons and unicorns. They don't know the stories that, from time immemorial, have allowed children to understand life and their own selves. Thank God for Luke Skywalker, but they have never heard of Odysseus or Theseus or Psyche, tales that would keep alive the itch for Eden in them. By the time they reach me, they are all too ready for the smart-ass *Weltschmerz* of Holden Caulfield and the winsome pessimism of Kurt Vonnegut.

Take children to the woods and to the beach, away from buildings and billboards, movies and Saturday cartoons, Trivial Pursuit and Monopoly. Ask if they can feel a presence there, something beyond the sigh of the wind and the harrumph of the waves. It will not improve their grades; it is more a test of what we teachers and parents truly hold important for our children.

Let children's liturgies be *fun*. For God's sake, don't preach to them. Let each one tell what God looks like; let each one tell "What I like about Sarah is . . ." Don't do it *for* them. Let the hymns be rousers, what we used to call "Negro spirituals," effusions that rouse both the natural and the supernatural sides of the soul. And at least by junior high, students should be ready for a weekend retreat—perhaps not yet a purely supernatural one, but one where they can break down their ego-defenses in safety, reach out, be vulnerable and unafraid for a while.

---

66 We have a duty to our students' minds, but we have a more profound duty to their souls. 99

In high school, we ought to give at least some time to the same kinds of activities. Granted, a few years ago, we belted the pendulum all the way from the preceptive catechism to the huggy-kissy-touchy-feely-group-grope, and since then have had to give religious education a kind of academic respectability again. But we have overcompensated. One such exercise is "trust," where one student falls backward and another catches him or her. I've seen boys who on Saturday skated ninety miles an hour, unfazed by being slammed into the boards, turn around maybe five times: "Now, you're *there,* right? If you *try* anything . . ." Paranoia even among pals. The difference between the hockey game and the exercise was that, on skates, the boy himself was *in charge.* How do we make such a boy vulnerable to God? Not overnight.

In senior year, I spend two quarters studying pop psychology with boys in religious ed. Except for an occasional comment, it's rarely overtly religious, and yet if I can't make them understand how to evolve an adult self, how can I ever stimulate their "teenage spirituality"? The moral self (*ethos,* character) is not separable from the spiritual self. Thus, we study how purely analytical, left-brain ideas are often half-witted, that we are all victims of the animal id and the superego taped from our socialization as children, unless we—at no small effort—wrestle for an ego: a self, a character, a personally validated ethic. We study Erikson's stages of development and the natural shocks we encounter as we grow, without which we remain children for life. We study not only the differences in sexuality but the androgynous (masculine/feminine) nature of souls, male or female. And we finish with the Enneagram, a study of nine basic personality types similar to but not as left-brain as the well-known Myers-Briggs test. (I have never seen any group of classes more sure-fire with seniors than the Enneagram. Even in the class after lunch, the somnambulists are bright-eyed and alert!)

Ironically enough, science teachers are especially able to break down the left-brain bias of students and open them to a sense of the numinous—provided they go beyond the confines of the cookbook syllabus. Physics was always the hardest of the "hard" sciences to most people, and still is: the extreme specialization of the analytical mind. From Democritus to Newton and beyond, it had a mechanistic concept of the world, a model in which matter was broken into basic building blocks, passive, leaden. It triumphed in the Cartesian dichotomy between the world (the *res extensa*) and the mind (the *res cogitans*). It was all very neat and predictable.

But since Heisenberg and Einstein and Planck, we know that mass—the hard-edged objects we heft and skin our shins against, the whizzing pellets in the atom—is not really *res extensae* at all! Mass is nothing but a form of energy. Atomic particles do not consist of any basic "stuff," but are bundles of "tendencies to exist." Electrons are both particles and waves at the same time, and there is only a strong probability of finding a particular particle in a particular place at a particular time. As elusive as God. In the four-dimensional continuum of space-time, you can't really ask how fast anything is going; the answer is valid only relative to where *you* happen to be standing at the moment. The physicist begins to sound like an Eastern mystic.

As Fritjof Capra wrote in the *Saturday Review* (December 10, 1977), both modern physics and Eastern mystics "emphasize that the universe has to be grasped dynamically as it moves, vibrates, and dances; that nature is not a static equilibrium but that it is a dynamic one." God and the universe are not nouns but verbs. Both the physicist and the mystic must be "able to attain nonordinary states of consciousness in which they transcend the three-dimensional world of everyday life to experience a higher, multidimensional reality. . . . The survival of our society will depend, ultimately, on our ability to adopt some of the *yin* ['feminine'] attitudes of Eastern mysticism, to experience the wholeness of nature and the art of living with it in harmony."

---

66 *Very young children are far better candidates for meditative, receptive, 'feminine' prayer than adults.* **99**

Most parents want their children to have "the good life," and they believe that a good college is the road to such a life, and the SATs are the narrow gate onto that road. Some spend large amounts of cash for special courses. If Capra is right, they might spend their money more wisely, in the long run, by teaching their children to meditate.

To achieve a teenage spirituality, we must first prove to our young the undeniable existence of their souls. Then perhaps we can show them the One for Whom those souls were made.

EIGHT

Toward an Adult Spirituality

Better a mop-wringer saint than a theologian sinner; more important to know *God* than know *about* God. Few would disagree, yet I wonder if in practice the Church reveres its retreat-givers and gurus as highly as its theologians, or even its administrators. I wonder, too, whether, just as most Christians left learning about God (theology) back in high school or college, they also left learning to know God better (spirituality) back in grade school or on their mothers' laps—if they learned it there.

Little doubt that schools and parents care about children's minds, or that religious educators and other teachers—as well as many parents—care about solving children's religious *problems,* but I wonder how many care about their religious *hungers,* about their souls. We all want to "save their souls," but I have a hunch that means saving their souls from hell in the future and not saving their souls from atrophy and mediocrity here and now.

Listening to and teaching adults, reading diocesan newspapers, I hear an understanding of God (what God cares about) and ways of praying that would not tax a child's mind, because the last time adults learned any theology or spirituality was as children, or at best in some college theology courses and perhaps a retreat. The difficulty is that a simplistic idea of God does tax the credulity of an adult—or should. God has no genitals; the hell-within is worse than Dante's; the soul is not satisfied merely by a dutiful Mass; Jesus didn't mention a penance, temporal punishment, or purgatory to the adulterous woman.

Two Questions

Every year the first two questions I ask kids are: (1) "How have your image of God and relationship with God changed since fifth grade?" (2) "How do your parents answer the question? If you want, simply have one write out the answer for you."

There have been interesting results in the one hundred plus times I've asked. A running tally shows consistently only three out of thirty actually ask; most guess; those who give reasons say they'd be embarrassed, or it'd be a hassle, or "we don't talk about that stuff." At least for the three thousand or so young men and women I've taught in four different cities, not much God-talk is heard at home.

I have no direct access to what parents believe or do about God, but one gets a suggestion of that from what their children at least perceive their parents believe and do, and from what the parents seem to have been able to pass on to their children.

The Young. The majority of kids assume their own image of God and relationship must have grown, as if understanding were as automatic and effortless as physical growth and despite the fact hardly any can make specific just how the image and relationship have changed.

Many confuse their relationship with God and their relationship with the Church, and what they describe as growth is actually a regression to sophisticated disdain.

Despite great strides in catechetics since we were their age, the majority of young people say growth consisted in rejecting the same "Old Man with a White Beard" most of us were also brought up on—the Super Entity who holds all the cards, loves and punishes, and yet with no successful attempt by parents or teachers to harmonize those two contrary activities. Though one or two in each class say their parents are embittered by the Job question ("How could a good God . . . ?"), I can't remember one who said parents or teachers gave even a tentatively satisfying answer.

Nearly all students, college and high school, say their last growth in knowing God was confirmation, at least five or six years ago. Those who have made a retreat say their spirituality made a significant advance, though the God they describe is almost always limited to awareness of "God-in-the-group." That is surely growth, but there is little sense that awareness continues in school or extends into parish Masses or into personal prayer.

When they mention prayer, it is often a rejection of "memorized prayers" and Mass, or a forthright admission they pray only in a jam, bargaining and maneuvering with God to change God's mind. Although a few in every group seem still to have a quite meaningful friendship with God, in those thousands of responses, not a single student said parents—or pastors or teachers—taught them how to pray as adults: centering themselves and listening.

Parents. Youngsters' suspicions of their parents' spirituality are varied but generally fall into three basic responses: they don't care, i.e., don't go to Mass, which is not evidence they don't know God; the strict old-time religion which seems at least to the youngster restricted exclusively to Mass; and a God who ultimately "pays us back" for pain expended.

All the answers actually written by parents are very childlike, simple, and moving, for me and for the student. Sad, so few students allow themselves and their parents to share, adult to adult (because they feel the parents don't *want* to), beliefs about what many still claim is the most important subject in our lives and, at the least, the sole reason parents pay tuition.

---

66 *Nearly all students, college and high school, say their last growth in knowing God was confirmation.* **99**

Thus, I can only guess from guesses my students' parents' beliefs: in most Catholic homes there is not much discussion of either theology or spirituality; where it does occur it is most often about doctrine rather than understanding God and about getting to Mass rather than knowing God better. This essay, then, is an attempt first to exhort parishes to consider courses in adult theology and spirituality for parents, and second to rough out at least for myself what the spirituality component of that course would consider. Though my direct dealings with adult spirituality are limited to summer courses and retreats, if I am a religious educator to the next generation of adult Catholics, I ought to find out what I'm preparing them for and how I should go about doing it. Physical education teachers instruct youngsters in "lifetime sports"; I ought to do something about lifetime praying.

Spirituality

What makes us human is not that we are rational animals; if that were so, we would be no more than what

reductionists claim: higher level animals. Our brains
(which we share with animals) can turn information into
knowledge, but it is only in our souls that we can achieve
some measure of *understanding.* Our brains can figure
out the causes of things, but only in our souls can we begin
to discover the *reasons* for things. What makes us human
and continually more humanizable is our souls—our
spirits, our selves, our who-I-am. Yet far too many
humanizable beings are never provoked even to become
aware of their souls (what makes them human), much
less understand them and bring them more alive.

Saint Paul says, "Unspiritual persons do not accept
anything of the Spirit of God, seeing it all as nonsense; it
is beyond their understanding because it can be understood only by means of the Spirit. Spiritual persons, on
the other hand, are able to judge the value of everything, and their own value is not judged by others."
Unspiritual people do not so much scorn the Spirit as
become insulated from it—by the rat race, by materialist
anesthetics, by the need for acceptability by others. And
even the omnipotent Spirit cannot enter the human spirit
uninvited. But as Christopher Koch writes in *The Year
of Living Dangerously:* "The spirit doesn't die, of course;
it turns into a monster."

Anyone can see a spectrum of humanity ranging from
sociopaths who savage women in parks to such splendid
spirits as More and Gandhi. Unlike our simian cousins,
we have the potential to be more than what we were born
as; unlike theirs, our nature is an invitation, not a command—an invitation always beckoning us further into
"that untraveled world whose margin fades / Forever and
forever as I move." Each time with no less pain.

Humanity is what Australian poet Les Murray calls
"degrees of acceptance of the Spirit." The journey of a
soul has (at least) five stages: the natural, this-world,
Wordsworthian sense of the numinous; the this-world
need to "make sense of it all"; the this-world urge to evolve
an adult conscience in order to be at the very least an

honorable human being; the hunger born in us—but not of this world—to reach beyond the limits of time and space to the Reality from which one's soul is a lonely emigré; and finally, that meaningless-to-the-world-beater demonic drive to expend what little life we have in service of our neighbor and our King. "You'll kill yourself working like that!" Fine.

The Numinous. That ability of the soul to quicken is lurking in any of us, no matter our supernatural sensibilities, just as the potential for parenthood lurks in our bodies. It is a presupernatural stage, not merely gush or emotion or greeting-card sentimentality, but a sense of wonder, awe, quest. It knows —beyond the need or ability to "prove"—value more vibrant than numbers, a resonance to the mystery and incongruity of the world. My father was never educated in music or literature or anything else but suffering and serving, and yet tears rimmed his eyes when he listened to classical music written by people whose names he had no need to know. We all feel it, surprised by stars, or a painting, or a baby. It bursts out in helpless laughter, which puts our tragedies into perspective, which forgives God, and which is—even in the unbeliever—an act of praise for the Great Surpriser who gleefully created the trilobite and the giraffe and the hairy-nosed wombat, in defiance of reason and efficiency.

Philosophy. There is in all of us also at least the potential to go beyond the dumb animal acceptance of things-as-they-are, to ask why things aren't "as they should be," the itch that moved every writer from the Genesis poet to Vonnegut to ask the never-ending question: "What the hell are people for?" But it seems the majority of human beings simply knuckle under to an unintelligible life sentence—or at least limit themselves to "beating the odds." The dull-eyed Man with the Hoe, third-generation welfare mothers, grim-faced social workers—like Boxer in *Animal Farm,* they adapt in noble futility to what they believe unchangeable: "The revolution is failing; I will work harder," never asking the uniquely human question: "Why?" But there are always a persnickety few, like Winston Smith in *1984*, who can't resist the primal temptation to stick their noses into books, to see if someone might have come up with a better answer.

---

66 *What makes us human and continually more humanizable is our souls.* 99

Conscience. There is a further potential in the human soul to take possession of one's own life and choices, to distance oneself from what "everybody says and does," to critique all the socializing messages parents, teachers, and the media have taped on the superego, to evolve an ego—a personally validated conscience—which enables one to say, legitimately, "I believe . . ." and not merely "They tell me . . ." We need a core of values with which to anchor our lives, values we can fine-tune as we learn more but can never reject. Instead of certitudes or stereotypes, we need directions for making choices. But that requires the considerable effort of thinking: gathering data, sifting it, putting it into some kind of logical sequence so that we can draw a conclusion and put it out to be tested. And that is what schools—public and private— do not teach, preferring the more expeditious "ingest-and-regurge" and objective testing of data students will never find use for, rather than challenging young people to go in quest of their own answers and reasons and selves. As a result, "conscience" becomes no more than watching which fork everybody else uses.

Transcendence.   Deeper than those nature-hungers is a far subtler call Augustine heard, to reach beyond the limits of time and space: "Our hearts are restless till they rest in Thee." Some souls, unsatisfied with *pro forma* ritual, commandments, and conformity, crave union with the energizing Spirit working in us at a level we barely apprehend, much less grasp. They hear a call *beyond* humanity, but still an invitation to which one must assent: "Be it done unto me according to your word."

Service.   "We love God because God first loved us." We own our giftedness and commit ourselves to embody our gratitude in service, to share the superaliveness. "Here I am. Send me."

The "world" is wiser than we. Its advertisers arouse a need in us, make us aware of what we're missing *before* they show us bogus ways to fulfill it. If we are to convert the young—and the not-so-young, we have a better chance if we try first to quicken their natural spirituality. But in most cases we really don't. And even if we did, if we claim to be schooling apostles, it would still not be enough. And so, like Boxer, we continue to teach a Christian doctrine the young have no felt need for and thus, when they become adults, will long since have forgotten.

The Limits of Natural Spirituality

The Numinous.   Even in itself, without any consciousness of its objectively supernatural Source, opening the soul to the numinous in nature and art is a profoundly enriching experience too many humanizable beings deny themselves—or are denied. It breaks out into a larger context of meaning and value, as Wordsworth said: "a sense of something far more deeply interfused"— which is, in fact, the presence of God whose name is "I AM." God is the pool of existence out of which everything-that-is draws its existence, the power who energizes everything that has "is," from the Great Silent Carouse of the universe to the sizzling heart of the tiniest particle, so that every hour of research is a prayer. Thus, exulting in the immanent richness of creation in and of itself is beautiful, yet it doesn't go far enough. It is a signpost, not the destination it tempts us toward. We are so in awe of the entryway, we fail to enter the banquet.

The icon focusing the presence of God becomes an idol, and religion regresses into aesthetics. What's more, we live in a cynical era in which even icons become bastardized or belittled: the American eagle hawks overnight mail; baseball is a business; the American myth devolves into the American dream and what someone has called "Californication" of value. The innate hungers of the human spirit can be palliated by ersatz pap: quasi-religious rock liturgies, saints, and sacramentals, which differ from Nazi rituals and symbols only as a different style of celebrating the same reality: paganism. Still, there remains one superb modern symbol which, like the crucifix, celebrates a nobility of spirit even in defeat: the Vietnam War Memorial.

This-worldly celebrations of the human spirit are often very beautiful and, even in vulgar embodiments, always very powerful. But there is nothing in them of the transcendent, the food the soul was made for, the only reality that can satisfy its hungers. This immanent world simply isn't enough, because there is death, and death is the only reality in our future we can make book on. Here again is the constant call of the seeking soul, this time in a more plaintive voice: "There's *got* to be more than this!"

Philosophy.   Nor is immanent understanding of what life is for enough to satisfy the soul because, again, there is death. Without a dimension to our existence beyond the four dimensions of time and space, without a life beyond this one, our undeniable hungers to know the ultimate why and to survive death—which specify our species and which we share with no other we know—will never be satisfied. Thus our very human nature is a curse.

Evolution made one accidental stumble too far and came up with the only species that knows its every effort is ultimately futile.

Conscience. Nor, except for rare and sublime souls like Camus, is immanent morality enough. There are surely men and women whose sole motive for greatness of soul is respect for their own inviolable integrity, without anchor or support from outside time and space. But for us weaker vessels, the pull of pragmatism is too powerful; we need reminding that Someone Else programmed the laws of physics into the stars, wrote the natures of rocks and food and animals and humans into their fibers, to tell us what ways we may legitimately use them. Our tenuous grip on truth needs validation from a Mind wiser and more farseeing than our own. For still weaker souls, as with the numinous, morality devolves even further into acceptable behavior and religion into another method of establishing respectability. Law replaces Spirit; conformity replaces commitment of the spirit to quest.

Supernatural Spirituality

It is easy for those sensitized to the "freshness deep-down things" to find God on a sunset mountain peak, or in a forest gauzed in mist, or in the desert where God is inescapable. But those who have never been led to find God in easy places are not likely to find God in difficult ones. As we go, we find God ambushing us all the time where we least expected, from what we had thought commonplace, ambushing not as enemy but as Hobbes ambushes Calvin every day after school: for the sheer damn fun of it! In my foolish years, I thought "contemplative in action" meant walking serenely through the poopstorm with the sound turned off, one's mind focused only on God speaking on the inner Walkman, just as I wrongly believed Jesus walked the roads of Palestine, impervious to the stink because he was unaware of it. No. It's *in* experiencing the action that we contemplate God, aware of more than surfaces, sensing the aliveness and connectedness of things, the energizing Spirit who gives things his "am," seeing them transfigured, no matter what their unpromising disguises, like bread and wine.

> 66 *Our tenuous grip on truth needs validation from a Mind wiser and more farseeing than our own.* 99

The goal, however, is to sensitize our souls to the presence of God in ever more difficult disguises: monotonous gray days, the boss often in error but never in doubt, meetings. I've found that when I go out with my good-guy glasses on, there is indeed no such thing as a bad boy. But I know my spirit still has much growing to do; there is no way I've found the trick of sensing God in Puritans, condescension, or courageous ignorance. But if God can send messages through orifices as unpromising as Balaam's ass, I suspect God's telling me something through them, too.

God may use angels with more privileged souls, but in my own case I find God uses Labrador retrievers too often for any doubt. On one occasion I was walking along a country road, just hangin' out with Jesus, when this Lab came up and nudged me with a stick. So I threw it till I got tired and stopped. She gave me a scowl and hipped me, as if I'd forgotten my place. Just then, a car came careening down the road and I grabbed her collar and yanked her back. She choked, coughed, snarled, and sulked away. It was an epiphany: I suddenly realized that I comprehended God's refusals and gifts of pain about as much as that dog comprehended mine. Humbling, but the truth. From a fat-bottomed old Lab.

Scripture. The Testaments also unfold our souls. Yielding place to God is a task we've balked at since Adam and Eve. The heroes God chose were almost universally not ones we would have picked: cowards, stammerers, drunks, turncoats, spindly shepherd boys and, in general, Cinderellas and nerds. God is not answerable to us. For reasons we will never comprehend here, God created a world where there could be hurricanes, cancer, deformed babies, and death, and gave freedom to an inadequately evolved tribe of apes. Pure and simple, we serve a God smitten with paradox, whose idea of winning is our idea of defeat: a cross. And the love of God very often seems the wrath of God—quite likely because the wrath of God *is* the love of God, assessed by a fool.

Nor is Jesus, the embodiment of God, the messiah we would have chosen. Quite unlike Hitler or the Stones or Hefner—who also changed the world, simply by intuiting which way the parade was heading and getting in front of it—Jesus did not give us a message we wanted to hear. He came to turn the parade in precisely the opposite direction; he spoke words hard for our canny hearts even to give credence to, much less heed: take the last place (the real parade is heading the other way), forget yourself (even your shortcomings), take up your cross, heal the hateful. "We piped, and you would not dance." So we killed him.

But we still try to remake Jesus to our image, not so daunting a challenge to our spirits, not just domesticating him into a blue-eyed goy or the exclusively protective Good Shepherd but, truckling to democracy, we change his "Kingdom" to "Realm," defusing monarchical over-tones. But he *is* a King, and the Kingdom he has ruled since before the beginning is not a democracy. If we dare admit the truth, he often is—or seems—capricious and despotic, not merely in the matter of people's swine and

Temple stalls, not merely jerking our own collars, but crushing the innocent and those we love. Anyone who has seriously read—or lived—the Book of Job does not soften "Kingdom" to "Realm."

I don't "sense" that is the kind of God most people I homilize to every Sunday or the people whose children I teach want to hear about. But it is a very real aspect of the God who is.

The Liturgy. The problem with dis-spirited liturgy is not primarily with a vacuous text or uninspired performance; the root is the edgy uptightness of the audience, spiritless—almost like dutiful servants invited up at Christmas to watch the gentry eat. No one sings full-throatedly without fear of seeming pious, if not hypocritical. If the congregation would lower its guard and let God in more often, if they truly *cared* about Mass, my hunch is they'd storm chanceries for something better than they're getting. Mass is no time for theologizing, for "class," for moving the mind—much less for sin-talk or fund-raising. It is time for liberating the soul. Time for communion.

Practica Quaedam

. If we want the next generation spiritually adult, let their parents, teachers, and pastors rediscover their own spirits. Exhort the young to read poetry, Shakespeare, and novels only if you do yourself. Exhort them to pray or go on retreat only if you do yourself. Do parents or teachers (outside religious education) read even a novel with some kind of theological or spiritual dimension and tell kids about it? Do teachers or parents tell youngsters how and when and why they pray? Or how their lives would be centerless without prayer? What we do shouts so loudly they can't hear our claims. Imagine the effect on a group of boys if a coach said he'd missed the first half hour of "Monday Night Football" because he hadn't had time to pray yet that day! Would they begin to believe our claims that our schools and parishes are genuine communities and all our teachers are apostles?

> **66** *We serve a God smitten with paradox, whose idea of winning is our idea of defeat: a cross.* **99**

Christ came for the sick, but most of us claim to be healthy—or at least OK. Until we admit our need, we will never admit our dependence; and until we admit our dependence, we will never seek the only Food to feed the deepest part of ourselves—not only the Eucharist but the "freshness deep-down things," Who is everywhere we turn, if only we had eyes sensitized to see and ears sensitized to hear. Even in a "boring" Mass. In impoverishing our own spirits, we impoverish the spirits of our children.

One final stunning paradox: in creating us free, the Omnipotent gave up some personal freedom so we could be free. Without our invitation, God cannot break through to us. If we don't acknowledge God's knocking, God must stay outside.

That's one crazy kinda God.

NINE

Who Is God?

Arrogant title for such a brief treatment. Ranged against me, I have merely the lifetime work of Augustine, Aquinas, Buddha, Muhammad, Teilhard (among others) on the one hand, and Voltaire, Madalyn Murray O'Hair, and Carl Sagan (among others) on the other. To speak nothing of an endlessly droning procession of druids, shamans, dervishes, gurus, vestal virgins, and devil worshipers. So you see it's quite an easy topic, one that I can easily fungo right out of the park.

The primary problem about God today, I think, is not *who* God is but *whether* God is. In the long run, to be frank, who needs God? Oh, the one whose kid or spouse or parent is in the I.C.U., of course. But over the long haul, we're all adults, right? And we're "cool." Since our earliest days with Monopoly and sandlot ball, we've all been trained not to let friend or foe see our weaknesses or our dependence. In the brainwashed paranoia of our times, one daren't let the enemy see the cracks in our defenses—and, to the paranoid, even one's best friend is a potential betrayer.

"Who needs God?" is, of course, a vacuous question if God is indeed *there.* If there is Someone who opened the door to existence—and to all the gifts that depended on that initial gift—then one ought to be grateful, though gratitude itself is a disconcertingly humbling and . . . well . . . "exposed" posture.

In the biblical story, Adam and Eve were the first to fall prey to the suspicion that God (though essential to the first leg-up) could easily be dispensed with after that, like the first essential but expendable stage of a rocket. Sort of like one's parents. Once one has "arrived," who needs God?

"Eat this, and you'll become like God." All it takes is that one self-assertive move, and we're free of Daddy's rule. Oedipus and Prometheus and Sisyphus got rather spinarty, too; they were going to show the gods that they'd outgrown them. However, if it's the objective truth—the nature of things—that God is God and we are God's creatures, then those who violate that truth will discover to their peril that truth inevitably rises up to take its revenge. Not the wrath of God, just . . . the-way-things-are.

And it always ends up the same way, doesn't it? Oh, not always with Adam or Oedipus or the prodigal son heading for home, hat in hand, submissive to the truth—to the way things are. There are those who stay away forever, impotently sophisticated enough to know that—even if life is now empty and absurd—one simply does not return to bend the knee. How degrading.

They tell me that one time when I was a kid, I walked to the john in my sleep. And although the results later proved that I was doing quite satisfactorily, my dad called out, "Is that you, Bill?" And—even in my sleep—I called back, "I can take care of *myself!*" The same is true, I think, with ourselves and God, our Father. We remain, in God's regard, perpetual adolescents: feisty, independent, cantankerous, even when we know our Father is right—*especially* when we know our Father is right.

We live in a generation deadly—and I use the word advisedly—afraid of awe. When does one dare to say "Wow!" or "Gasp!" out loud? It's the Age of Cool, and cool cannot confess the dependence and vulnerability (and surely the inferiority) that the word *Wow!* admits to. That would be to surrender to the unspoken judgments of all those around us about our inadequacies. Awe brings us to our knees, and we look very small and vulnerable on our knees.

Children, on the other hand, are blissfully naive. They stand in awe of a knock-kneed old nag daydreaming in front of a junk wagon. *We* can't even stand—in awe—of our friends and parents and siblings. What can evoke awe (which betokens humility) today? A man walking a tightrope between the two buildings of the World Trade Center? Perhaps. But life itself has been trivialized. And death. And sex. We've forgotten the taste of bread. We've left behind the awe we felt at the unexplored grass at the edge of the baby blanket. We need a different kind of grass now. We've eaten of the Tree of Knowledge of Good and Evil, and we've grown up. We're more "grown up" than God.

And there is no *time* for awe—or peace, or solitude. There is always too much to be done. And without God it's all on *our* shoulders, isn't it? Without God, all we can do is be afraid of the inevitable.

Who is God? God's the one who opened the door, who invited us to the ball. Obviously, if we'd never *come* to the ball, we'd never have known what we missed. But we *are* at the ball, and, my God, it's so beautiful! But we get so involved in griping about the trappings and shortcomings of the ball that we forget that we need not have been invited at all. Very often, we even forget to thank the Host for inviting us.

If anyone asks me why young people—and their progenitors—don't go to Mass, or else go with dull and sheepish servitude, I think I have the answer—a double-barreled answer. Number one, they've been spoiled so rotten they think being spoiled is an incurable disease. And, number two, as I said to my dad, "I can take care of myself!" What an awesome burden: to believe one must succeed where God has failed.

---

66 *Awe brings us to our knees, and we look very small and vulnerable on our knees.* **99**

You know all the notional, academic, second-hand, catechism answers to the question: Who is God? You know all *about* God. The greater question is: Do you know *God?*

The Judeo-Christian God

We've all been exposed to the Judaeo-Christian God, even though the Bible remains the most-sold and least-read book on earth. We learn of God from the worst of sources: Hollywood pseudobiblical epics, obscenely saccharine holy cards, and the homogenized plaster icons in most churches. God is *either* the thundering Jehovah, who's going to whup our sinful tushes, *or* the Good Shepherd, who's going to pat our woolly heads and make everything nice again—depending, I suppose, on one's blood father. God is Charlton Heston and Max von Sydow, with a touch of David Bowie. We imprison the limitless God within those bunkum boxes! And yet even the breathtaking images of Chartres ultimately wither when compared to their Subject.

The Jews were wise. They wouldn't allow anyone to draw a picture of God, just as J. D. Salinger won't allow anyone to play Holden Caulfield on the screen. To concretize the real-but-not-tangible God is very simply to negate God's immensity—except insofar as Jesus embodied God. How does one physicalize the Being who is captured inadequately even by such asbestos-souled initiates as Moses and Paul and Teresa of Avila, who described God as fire and unapproachable light?

And yet—with a whimsicality one sees more and more—God nonetheless became physical in a baby lying in straw amid the dung smell, and in a felon slaughtered on a gallows. Compounded, as we are, of spirit and flesh, symbols are essential for us—if we are to deal at all with the intangibles of love, honor, God. But we inevitably fall into the trap of thinking we've locked God into our symbols and formulas. Then, perversely, the symbols begin to take on the holiness—perhaps even the reality— of God. The iconoclasts weren't total fools; the icons can become idols. To say that "God doesn't look like that at all" becomes, to the simpleminded, nearly heresy. It threatens the simple faith of all of us, especially if we've taken physics and anthropology and psychology.

The God of Other Religions

Nor, despite our temptations to parochialism, is our God a different being from the God of other religions. The Buddhists may etherealize God too close to nonexistence for my taste, and the pagans may smash God up into a thousand component godlets, but it's the same God. It's the same God—filtered through a different prism, whom the Muslims adore when they bow toward Mecca.

It's the same God the pantheists sense under the skin of everything that imprisons life. It's the same God to whom the aborigines bow in the waterfall. Like the blind men in the Calcutta park who've discovered the disparate parts of an elephant, each religion sees only part of the Infinite Being. But the inadequate mumbles of each can enrich the apprehension and discovery of all the others. If they'll only stop arguing and listen to one another.

The God of the Physicist

However, the one insight into God which I think we have heeded too little is the insight of the physical scientist. One discovers the personality of the Artist—communes with God—through God's creations, and few have a richer view of that exciting "freshness deep-down things" (who is God) than the modern physicist.

I think back to the days when, despite two and a half years of atomic physics, my prayer was still locked back into the symbols of Ptolemy and Dante, when I prayed through the limitless cold of space to the Celestial Jerusalem where God lives, fanned by the wings of fiery-cheeked cherubim. It never struck me how many light-years it would have taken the hermaphroditic Gabriel to cross that gulf from God to Nazareth, or the wear and tear on his/her feathers, or the sheer exhaustion with which he/she delivered his/her message. It never crossed my mind that if Jesus went "up" from Jerusalem at the Ascension, an old Mongolian lady would have to go in precisely the opposite direction when she went "up." Somehow, I kept Albert Einstein in one lobe of my brain, and Cecil B. DeMille in the other. And the right-hand brain never told the left-hand brain what it was doing.

The crunch came when I had to give a homily on the Ascension just after my ordination. (Remember, now: I was thirty-three at the time!) I hate to give the same old poop, so I decided to meditate on the event as concretely as I could. So. I saw the field and the little knot of people coming into it. Jesus said good-bye and started rising. It was OK for the first fifteen feet or so—up to the point where the portraits usually freeze the frame. But I decided to let it run. And he went up. And up. Did he go through the Van Allen belt? Was he radioactive? Did he move serenely by the planets and out into the cold of space—out, out . . . until he finally came to the thin, thin membrane that separates God's way of existing from the physical universe? And then, did he go through it—boooop!—as through a self-sealing tire, into heaven? Back to the drawing board on that one.

❝Who is God? You know all about God. The greater question is: Do you know God? ❞

So God (I'm sure it was God) manipulated my thoughts toward black holes. Without provoking the slightest derision, Carl Sagan says anything caught near the vortex of a black hole would be spun out into an infinitely thin line, down into a kind of celestial sewer. But where would this entrapped thing end up, one asks? And Carl Sagan answers, without batting one lash, "In another universe." Ah, Carl. You just played to my trump! Suddenly, my hard-pressed faith was no longer locked into the symbols available to first-century cosmology. What Jesus did at the Ascension was to go through a time warp, if you will, into another way of existing, into a dimension of reality where time and space have no meaning—where we are merely shadows, of imitations, of Reality.

Since then, I find that science fiction helps me to visualize the realities of that way of existing better than the Johannine New Jerusalem, with its golden streets. (Where do they mine the gold? With what do they stoke the fires of hell? No energy shortage there, to be sure.) Even science fiction taxes no one's imagination in presenting "presences" that are intelligent but not four-limbed—shining globes or shimmering lights that speak.

Thus, when I pray now, God has no beard. He doesn't even look like the Jewish Jesus. God is "a Person made of light."

In liberating myself from the limitations of the first-century symbols, I found the physicist's imagination let me concretize the realities of religion—still inadequately, of course, but less *in*adequately than the heavy concreteness of scriptural images.

Perhaps the scriptural images are sacrosanct to archivists, traditionalists, and other purists. But I'm trying to hang on to a very precarious faith—not in the Roman Catholic Church, or even in Christianity, but in the very existence of God. And I'm clinging to my vulnerability to God in a very invulnerable, "cool," sophisticated, materialist, and ungodly world that tells me I am quite naive.

Like astral physics, subatomic physics helps, too. Since Heisenberg, no one has dared suggest that the atom actually looks like the whizzing-pellet model we are all used to. That image is no more like a real atom than the old man on the throne is like the real God. Heisenberg showed that an electron sometimes acts like a pellet, and sometimes acts like a wave. Which is it? Neither, of course. But we know it's there—just as anyone who's unafraid to be caught being vulnerable knows that God is there.

You can't see an atom, only its effects on a photographic plate—its calling card. Similarly, we can't see God, only God's effects. The universe isn't a bad bit of evidence of something. We want God to pull off a few tricks and answer our prayers—when God has already pulled off a trick as stunning as the universe. But which of us would dare be caught being impressed?

Physicists tell me that, at the innermost core of the nucleus of an atom, the most fundamental components may not be extended at all. Like God. The parts are moving so fast that they seem to be at rest. Like God. They're moving with such lack of inhibition that they're everywhere at once. Like God. As Hopkins wrote, "The world is charged with the grandeur of God." God is burning under all the surfaces. We are in God's presence at every moment, all-unknowing, as Helen Keller was in the sunshine. The only thing we'd have to sacrifice to know God is our pretensions to God's job.

We are immediately aware only of a four-dimensional reality: space and time. But if there is a fifth dimension to reality—a transcendent dimension in which God and those who have survived death exist—then we are *in* that fifth dimension *now!* We don't begin to exist in it after death. It's a dimension of *this* life. We are in it now, thoroughly permeated by it—just as we're permeated by gamma rays without our being aware of them. If Jesus Christ freed us from the fear of death, then we're immortal *now.* That's what we celebrate every Sunday— unless we take waking up in the morning for granted, as if we deserved it.

We get intimations of that other dimension of our lives in moments of ecstasy, of awe, of prayer—for those who dare to be vulnerable to ecstasy, and awe, and prayer. At those privileged times, we are "out of ourselves," unaware of the four confining dimensions of space and time. We're freed of the one thing that keeps us from God: our paranoid narcissism.

The Personality of God

Who is God? God is the Infinite Other—in our midst. Each of us sees I-Am through his or her limited and unique prism. I can go to any man or woman, living or dead, and say, "Tell me about God." Even the atheist can tell me how ultimately empty, sterile, and absurd the universe is without God. The deist and the Platonist (who seem to me to put God too far away and unapproachable) can nonetheless tell me about God's awesome holiness and blazing perfection. And *their* overbalance can be corrected by listening also to the pagan and pantheist (who seem to me to lock God too limitingly within the wonders of the Creator's works). *They* can remind me of God's humbling intimacy and aliveness burning beneath the surface of each everyday thing I touch. Even—if I'm humble enough to accept it—within me.

And the Hebrews can tell me about the God who has a perverse penchant for the Cinderellas—for the unpromising. Surely, if I were seeking the parents of the nation of Israel, the first couple I'd choose would be Abraham and Sarah, right?—both in their seventies and barren as a pair of bricks. Surely, if I had to bring down Goliath, I'd pick a spindly shepherd kid with a slingshot, right? And, my God, who'd ever have stuck that long with the grumbling, stumbling, griping, Baal-hungry people of Israel? Oh, but God has eons of time to wait for us to find our senses.

---

66 The only thing we'd have to sacrifice to know God is our pretensions to God's job. 99

Surely, if I were having a worldwide talent contest for the mother of the Son of God, I'd go to Athens first, and Rome, and Alexandria. Who would start in a no-name village, in a no-name province, with an illiterate hillbilly girl? You guessed it.

God's apparently smitten with nobodies—has the most intimidating jobs for nobodies. Better not say you're a nobody. It's about as safe as holding up a nine iron in a lightning storm. God's on the *prowl* for you nobodies.

And if Jesus Christ is the embodiment of God, he surely can tell us what God likes and dislikes. If you really have the guts to look, almost all the things God dislikes are the things the media have taught us to crave. And all the things God likes are the things they've taught us to run from as from lepers, whores, and tax collectors.

And the universe tells us about God's personality, what God likes and dislikes, just as any artwork reveals the personality of the artist. Look at the Great Dance of the planets—each turning on itself in an apparently lonely pirouette, and yet also turning around something else, and that union turning again around something else. Then go to the opposite extreme: a droplet of ditch water under a microscope. And what do you find? The same dance! The rigid plan of the periodic table and the laws of physics. You can't possibly get *law* from dumb *luck!* It begins to look like a plan. Nearly like a conspiracy.

But the Choreographer seems to like surprises, too. On the periodic table, those rare earths stick out so embarrassingly—almost as if the Artist were trying to keep Reality from becoming too regimented and the critics from becoming too snotty. God seems to love not only order but surprises. Every season follows the other, inexorably, and yet no two are alike. In all of Antarctica, the pattern of every snowflake is absolutely the same— and absolutely unique. In 300,000 years of human beings, DNA has never repeated itself even once. Order—and surprise.

We can ignore God, as we can ignore air and water, sunsets and spring, our eyesight and our lives—until they are threatened. And they all will be threatened, by suffering and by death. Those are God's two most painful surprises. For reasons we are not privy to, God is not answerable to us. The Creator invented a world in which there could be hurricanes and floods, in which—through no human moral failure at all—the innocent suffer. God allows a universe in which children can be born maimed, in which they can die in freakish accidents, in which any one of us can languish for years with wasting disease. The Almighty is not only the God of the Saint Louis Jesuits' hymns but also the God of Job.

At those times, when God's face—and reasons—are hidden in darkness, I really bawl God out, as I would any other friend who had betrayed my trust. I give God the whole works for doing something so demonstrably unfair. And then, as with any other friend, I forgive God. For the good times. "For the leaping greenly spirits and a new blue dream of sky," for babies and books and beer, for the people I've loved. And, in my few moments of wisdom, I realize that—without death—I'd take them all for granted, as if I'd done something to deserve them.

God's everywhere, Helen Keller, drawing signs in your uncomprehending hands. God is trying to penetrate your blindness, your Oedipal self-sufficiency, the smallness and smugness and security of the world you're tempted to settle for.

"Though the light has come into the world, we have shown that we prefer the darkness" (John 3:19).

All we have to do in order to see God . . . is to break all our mirrors. But, ah! What a price!

The hope that sustains me is that when we come to the end and see no longer through a glass, darkly, but finally face-to-face, we'll find ourselves saying, "Oh, my God! It was you all the time."

TEN

Jesus, the Warm Fuzzy

If I can choose my hell, it will be Dante's, not Sartre's. Painful, to be sure, but at least filled with high drama, what with all those archfiends doing such intriguing things to archiepiscopal hindquarters. Better, surely, than *No Exit.* Now there is a truly diabolical hell. I can think of at least ten people I would *not* want to spend all eternity cooped up in a room with—without hope of sleep, surcease, or suicide.

Similarly, if I had to choose my persecution, it would be the Roman kind, not the one I have. Gasping my last in a lion's jaws is a rather painful—not to say stuffy—kind of death, but at least there would be a sense of heroism, dignity, drama. Instead, the Enemy has visited upon me a far more diabolical persecution: being ignored.

In my innocent youth, religious educators had clout. They had the keys of the Kingdom of Heaven in one hand, with the other hand hovering over the button that triggered the trapdoor to hell. That's no longer true. Since one's death is now at best a myth and at worst an event so far in the future as to be dismissible, the Kingdom of Heaven (which may or may not follow that event) is equally dismissible. So, too, with hell—which nobody believes in anymore anyway. As a result, the religious educator has come full swing: from regulator to irrelevance.

Perhaps it's time for us to face an undeniable fact: Being a Catholic is no longer a very interesting proposition, and becoming a full-time professional at it (as a priest or religious) is, for most young people after the age of puberty, completely repellent. For too long we've contented ourselves with laying the blame for this disinterest solely on Hugh Hefner and Madison Avenue, on the dilution of Catholicism as its members were assimilated into the mainstream of a pluralist and materialist society. Ah, no! We have only ourselves to blame: bishops, homilists, elementary and high school religious educators, parents. We've short-circuited the power of the gospel. We've turned Jesus into a Warm Fuzzy.

Those 140,000 reflection papers have given me a pretty thorough—if disheartening—insight into the American Church of the nineties. Ten years ago, a student wrote: "I treat God as I would any adult." He had captured the feeling for God of the overwhelming majority of the students I've taught: respectful distance. They treat God as they would one of their parents' friends and the weekly visit to God's house like an obligatory stop at the home of a very rich distant relative. They're hardly eager to probe the life of their parents' Friend, hardly willing to stick around and listen to chitchat once dinner's over, and hardly ready to let that Friend have much heavy input into their decisions about their careers or their basic values unless they're going into that Friend's line of work. And this Friend is, after all, invisible, distant, and consistently silent.

Another question: Will your choice of career be in any way affected by your belief in Christianity? About 80 percent answer forthrightly in the negative. What could one possibly have to do with the other? Church is church, and business is business. The rest, who seem at first to answer positively, say that Christianity will certainly affect their career choices, "I mean, I'm not gonna be a pimp or a pusher or anything"—as if being Christian were merely a limitation on choices and not a challenge.

---

66 The religious educator has come full swing: from regulator to irrelevance. 99

The root of that notion, I think, is unearthed in the answers to still another question: What *is* the core message of Christianity—the irreducible elements without which one cannot call himself or herself a Christian? In all those years, after what students themselves call twelve years of "brainwashing," I can't recall a single student saying, "to be and act like a son of God," or "to be an apostle," or even "to be a person for others." What they describe as the core of Christianity is, rather, a kind of ethical "niceness" which would leave Christianity completely undifferentiable from the Boy Scouts or the Lions Club. Being Christian is, at rock bottom, not even to be generous to others but rather "as long as you don't hurt anybody else." In other words, being a Christian means being merely well-mannered—un-bad.

One's image of God is far more important than one's idea of God, because symbols capture invisible realities more satisfyingly than ideas do. When asked what their image of God is, many young people say "a kind of Force" as in "May the Force be with you." Such a Force is, of course, impersonal, mindless, and therefore undemand-ing. Or "George Burns in *Oh, God!*" As one student put it: "I have—and still have to some degree—the assumption that you can treat God like a wimp. Like I can do whatever I want, and God will just forget about it, no matter how I really feel. I felt I could really mess up, but it'd be no problem. It really isn't possible to have a relationship with a wimpy God."

In reacting against the overly restrictive and punitive God many of us were introduced to in our own childhood, we have swung full cycle in the other direction—from Moloch to Milquetoast. The God we encounter in homilies and in the hymns we mumble and moan on Sunday is almost exclusively the Good Shepherd who will pat our woolly heads and make everything nice and peaceful. We bowdlerize the Scriptures of anything that might be unpleasant or unsettling like "It is not peace I come to bring, but a sword." The Lamb of God has swallowed the Lion of Judah.

Symbols and images capture invisible realities far better than ideas and concepts do, and the image the next generation's Church has of Jesus (and therefore of God) does not originate in the New Testament. It comes from the liturgy and homilies, from mediocre-to-bad holy cards and church art, and primarily and most lastingly from biblical movies.

Consider the new Sacramentary. Only a liturgist could find any single segment moving. Like the hymns that accompany them, the prayers are bland, like creamed codfish on mashed potatoes. Not a single note to stir the heart, to challenge torpor, to ignite apostles. The young say, "It never changes." It does, of course, but it's so uniformly dull and distant from their own lives that it's difficult to tell the difference from one week to the next.

For them, then, it all depends on the homily. Some are lucky; most say they are not. If the tone is soporific or the presentation rambling, so is Jesus. If the content is top-of-the-head, innocuous, unchallenging, so is Jesus. If the homilist dodges the thornier aspects and goes for the consoling, if he tries to make it look easy, effectively denying the very words of Christ that being a Christian means carrying a cross—daily—then the gospel is made to appear flaccid, effeminate, spineless. And so is Jesus.

Most Catholics get their physical image of Jesus not from the New Testament but from art and films which are, in a word, *foma:* comforting lies. The Jesus of even the best biblical films, like Zeferelli's *Jesus of Nazareth,* doesn't even look human, much less male: long tapering fingers, skin pale as smoke, blue eyes glistering back into his head. Jesus seems "disconnected" and aloof among those smelly, stubbly apostles, like a priggish Oxford professor caught slumming. Thus, I'm not surprised that young or old wouldn't be particularly anxious to hear what such an abnormal being might say, or that they would be reluctant to invite him home for Sunday brunch after Mass.

The real flesh-and-blood Jesus simply could not have looked like that spindly mutant on so many holy cards. In the first place, he was a Jew. Look at the eyes and skin of Israelis and Arabs who live outdoors in Palestine. In the second place, he was a carpenter for twenty years. Look at a carpenter's hands. It is even more difficult to imagine such a man scourged with leaded whips, roughed up by the soldiers, cuffed through the screaming crowds, enduring spikes in his wrists and ankles—and taking three more hours to die.

Thus, image governs attitude (and vice versa). The Jesus of inexpensive religious art is so unworldly that one could not in any realistic way use him as a model for life as a *human* being. As a result, the Warm Fuzzy Jesus— and his message—become irrelevant, unchallenging, dismissible.

How could the young make a hero out of an effeminate irrelevance? (Note that I do not say "feminine."

Jesus was most laudably that. By "effeminate," I mean an overfeminized, undermasculinized male.) Jesus certainly said, "I am meek and gentle of heart" and "Turn the other cheek," but those were not the *only* things he said—or did. To do justice to those who hanged Christ, their motive was not that he was a gentle preacher who just wanted everybody to be nice. You don't hang an irrelevance. He claimed to be the Son of God, and he wouldn't shut up about it, even under threat of death. They didn't execute him because he was a bore; they thought he was too dynamic to be around, so dangerous that in the end Peter himself found it safer to claim he'd never known him.

---

66 *Symbols and images capture invisible realities far better than ideas and concepts do.* 99

Even to those who loved him, Jesus was unnerving. Surely, he was gentle to the sick, the oppressed, the overburdened. But he hung around in some very disreputable company—whores, tax collectors, sinners of all sorts—and what's worse, he even sought them out. He had little deference for men of wealth and social position, making rather imprudent jokes involving camels and needles. He cleared the whole Temple with nothing but a whip of small cords and his own blazing indignation. He had the audacity to speak up, routinely, to the equivalent of our priests' senate—*episcopo praesente*—and call them "frauds, self-aggrandizers, fit for hell, blind guides, whitewashed tombs, and brood of vipers," among other uncomplimentary things. I can't recall anywhere in the Gospels where Jesus bawls out any other human being, no matter how depraved, *except* the clergy: the elders of Judaism and his own seminarians.

Even his doctrine itself was unsettling. Jesus told a bunch of nobodies and cowards: "*You* are the light of the world!" He told them they had to climb up and shout what they'd heard from the rooftops. Always he kept telling them to stop worrying—about their clothes, about their height, about who was Number One. Forget that; in fact, forget yourself entirely, lose yourself in serving all the others. Take the last place. Put everyone else's needs ahead of your own. And in the end, there will be only one question to determine whether your life was worth living or a waste: "I was hungry, I was thirsty. What did you do about that?"

The frightening challenge of Christianity is embodied most startlingly in the crucifix. Can one look at it and say, "There is *the* most perfectly fulfilled human being who ever lived, at the moment of his greatest triumph. I want to be like him."

If Jesus or his gospel are boring, then I don't know what "interesting" means. And if the young don't find Jesus and his gospel unnerving, then I suspect they've never really heard them.

ELEVEN

Scripture from Scratch

If I gave copies of *The Exorcist* to an intelligent, sensitive high school class, and no student was scared for a single instant, I'd begin to wonder. If I then gave them *Helter Skelter,* and they weren't in any way disturbed, I'd begin to worry. If I then gave them *Waiting for Godot,* and they weren't confused or upset, I'd begin to get really scared. I would have to suspect that (1) they hadn't read the books, or (2) they'd read them so many times the books had lost their ability to shock, or (3) their receptivities were burned out by TV and loud music, or (4) their self-defensive barriers against unnerving truths were massive. Even the possibility of demonic possession, or ritual slaughter of innocent people, or the utter futility of human life and endeavor should make anyone above Cro-Magnon sensibility at least a *touch* uneasy. As a teacher, I'd feel compelled to seek the source of that insensitivity and do something about it.

And yet every day, all across the country, teachers give the Gospels to intelligent, sensitive students, and they don't bat a lash. They aren't scared; they aren't disturbed; they aren't confused or upset. They can blithely read that they should sell all they have and give it to the poor, yield first place to everyone else and take the last place, love God and the neighbor with the same sensitive concern they have when they look at themselves in the mirror—and it doesn't unnerve them in the slightest. All of that happened long, long ago in a galaxy far, far away. It makes one wonder if they would have snored through the Sermon on the Mount.

Something is radically wrong, and yet-most religion teachers I know seem to react to it with a kind of resigned frustration: "Maybe I'll get a film. Show them pictures of the Holy Land."

And thus the shattering Revolutionary of Nazareth is deflated—by one means or other—into a namby-pamby do-gooder who can be safely dismissed with the other losers.

It's an axiom of salespeople (and when you're dealing with baptized but not yet converted young people, every teacher, parent, and pastor becomes most definitely a salesperson): If the pitch fails, you dismiss the pitch-person. We, on the contrary, have the irritating habit of dismissing the audience. It is our job to find some way to get *this* message through to *this* audience. As Jerome Bruner said years ago, you can teach anything, in a meaningful way, to any audience, at any age, provided you can find a way to adapt it honestly to *their* receptivities. Very obviously, we haven't yet found that way to sell the Scriptures, not only to our young but to their parents. No homilist would be impoverished by offering a dollar to everyone in church who had read the Bible even ten minutes the previous week.

Somehow the fundamentalists manage to do that with many of our former Catholic high school and college students. They plant the raw gospel in front of young people, in the same uncompromising way Mark did, and dare them to confront themselves before that message and before Jesus Christ. It's primitive; it's without the slightest nuance; its converts seem utterly incapable of reasoning about it with compromise—or with humor—but it works! And its converts become nearly mono-maniacal about it, ablaze with the apostolic spirit, facing mockery and sneers without the slightest apparent anger—somewhat like the early Christians. On the contrary, I would dare parents and teachers to pose a (rather underhanded) dilemma to their young which I pose to mine, after eleven years of Christian "brainwashing": If someone offered you full college tuition and a $75,000 job after graduation in exchange for your standing up on TV and denying your faith in Jesus Christ, would you do it? The results are dispiriting, but if it's the truth, we're fools not to face it.

One could wonder if scholarship and theologizing and demythologizing—despite all their laudable effects—haven't left the Lion of Judah with his claws clipped. One could wonder if, as with the liturgy, we haven't homogenized Jesus of Nazareth into "a patient etherized on a table."

I'm surely not advocating fundamentalist simplism, nor a return to the James Joyce retreat. But I do think we have had too much of the meek and gentle Jesus and too little of the Galilean firebrand who said he'd come to bring not peace but a sword. One cannot suspect that most of the inhabitants of our high school or college classrooms or our Sunday pews see him that way. Our Lord is a marvelous role model for the children. It's just too bad he lived so long ago, in such simple times. He clearly didn't foresee how complicated things were going to get.

Furthermore, most of the stories in the New Testament now appear to be myths. All those tales about walking on water and demons and multiplying things are gross exaggerations. What with science and everything . . . well, I mean . . . one isn't naive. Or surely one doesn't want to *appear* to be.

Besides the vapidness of their understanding of the gospel, another reason for its ineffectiveness is that even when it is understood as a genuine call to knowing God and to apostleship, it seems all well and good for an ideal world, but it's surely impracticable for the very unideal world we have to live in: the all-pervasive rat race, the impersonal stampedes of our cities, the enormity of the information glut. Most of our energies are swallowed up in the frantic effort just to keep our heads above the maelstrom. If there are any minimally freed moments, we aren't in the mood for pondering the imponderables. Reach for the anesthetizing tube. Learning methods of prayer to contact God personally or deepening one's cognitive understanding of God by reading doesn't even make it onto the priority list. And yet parents still have to teach their children—with what they half remember from college or even from high school. Like the Deposit of Faith, learning about God was "closed" back then. The idea of *enriching* one's perception of Jesus and his message seems as silly as enriching one's perception of one's spouse after twenty years. C'mon! And if I probed any further, it might lead to doubt, and doubt is the second-worst sin.

> **❝ We have had too much of the meek and gentle Jesus and too little of the Galilean firebrand. ❞**

Still another reason Scripture has so little effect on Catholics lies precisely in ignorance of the true meaning—and necessity to human life—of symbol and myth. This is partly due to the bias of our educational institutions, which place such a lopsided emphasis on the rational as opposed to the intuitional, the SAT skills as opposed to sensitivity to nuance. We are frightened—or at least skeptical—of the nonquantifiable, the evanescent, the numinous, the imaginative. Therefore, much of religious education follows suit and becomes a rational argument and debate, principally on moral and doctrinal "issues." No problem with that; you need a rational defense of your faith: an apologetic. But the faith *life* can't survive on reason alone. Meanwhile, the Savior and the scriptural documents that started all this fuss in the first place are lost in the fog, "where ignorant armies clash by night."

This insensitivity to the true function of symbol and myth is critical. It is a major cause, I think, of the pseudointellectual rejection of the gospels as naive, a tissue of inane fabrications. The simplism of both credulous fundamentalism and cynical scientism fastens on the symbol *as if the symbol were the reality it only inadequately embodies.* This is, of course, as palpably foolish as saying the rose that stands for my love *is* my love and, when the rose wilts, my love has wilted.

And yet how many people feel their faith shaken—or even shattered—when they discover Gabriel didn't really need all those feathers to get from "way out there" to Nazareth? Or that a snake really didn't spend time chattering away to a naked lady in the park? Obviously, the author of Genesis didn't expect his audience to take him literally, any more than Aesop, writing at about the same time, thought his audience believed foxes and donkeys talked. But when the admittedly inadequate symbol is threatened, the *truth* is thereby threatened. If the snake didn't talk, there goes Genesis! And original sin! And the whole damn shootin' match!

These, then, are at least some of the apparent causes for the ineffectiveness of the Scriptures in most Catholics' lives: homiletic dilution to ethical humanism, the seeming impracticability of the Scriptures in the world of monopoly capitalism, the near cessation of religious learning at the end of one's formal education, and—at the root— ignorance of the true meaning and necessity of symbol and myth in human life.

The Root Problem

The taproot of ignorance and "rejection" of the Scriptures is not ill will on the part of religious educators. It is, if anything, an excess of goodwill and a paucity of common sense. Everybody wants to give the audience the whole ball of wax all at once. Nobody wants to begin with baby steps. It's the same with English: who wants to teach kids how to diagram a sentence? Let's get to the stories. The kids like them better.

I first came out to teach armed with a master's thesis on Dostoevsky's vision of human nature. I'd gotten an A plus for it. It was terrific. Having been condescended to as a high school student, I was gonna give *my* juniors the real stuff! So I dumped *Crime and Punishment* on them. Disastrous. It took me a while to realize I wasn't there to teach what excited me but what my students needed. Humbling. (Math teachers are much humbler than religious education or English teachers. And much more patient.)

Many teachers are similarly so enthusiastic over their subject matter that they forget how many years it took them to achieve even a rudimentary understanding of why the "stuff" was really important—much less any eagerness to dig more deeply into it. That enthusiasm leads them, unwittingly, to cater to their own interests and needs and not the real interests and needs of the potential converts they are missioned to serve.

This problem is typified, painfully, in the way teachers offhandedly use the concept of myth—which can be heady wine for a person who for years winced at boobish literalism or fretted over the seeming contradictions of Scripture. But this need for giant steps and aversion to baby steps infects not just the teacher bubbling home from a liberating summer course, but also—with far wider effects—seminary and graduate professors. When I was on sabbatical fifteen years ago, I overheard a dinner conversation between two profs who were heatedly debating the impenetrable ignorance of one of their third-year theology students: "He just can't seem to get it through his thick head that the resurrection is a myth. He keeps *fighting* it!"

Blinded by scholarship, they were overlooking several unsettling truths: (1) that the thick-headed seminarian in question had entered theological studies with a Ph.D. in physics; (2) that, as Paul said, if Jesus didn't rise from the dead, our faith (not to mention the seminarian's poverty, chastity, and obedience) is vain; and (3) that no one had ever troubled to show this accomplished young man just what they meant by the term *myth*.

**66 *Much of religious education . . .
becomes a rational argument and
debate, principally on moral and
doctrinal 'issues.'* 99**

Perhaps the profs assumed someone else had. To the young seminarian, as to *Time* and a good many unabridged dictionaries, *myth* means a person or idea existing only in the imagination, with no objective reality whatever, as in "the myth that a hat on a bed brings bad luck." No one wants to begin with baby steps.

Teaching Scripture to someone who has never understood the truth-bearing functions of symbol and myth is as demonstrably stupid as teaching *A la Recherche du Temps Perdu* to someone ignorant of French vocabulary or grammar. But we do it.

Myth is a story or theory that attempts to embody something *true,* but beyond literal, photographic description. Genesis, for instance, is a myth. It was written at least 300,000 years after the events it describes, not by an eyewitness. Barring divine implantation of the scenario, it consists of a series of surprisingly sophisticated educated guesses about the genesis of the earth and about the nature of human psychology. It attempts to embody something true (things obviously got here somehow; human beings are the only imperfect creatures). As such, both the theory of evolution and the science of psychology are also themselves myths: inadequate but usable symbol systems. All three have their loopholes and simplifications, but that does not negate their effectiveness, any more than loopholes and simplifications negate the effectiveness of the myth of progress or the myth of American democracy. The myth may be inadequate, but better than no attempt at all.

The atomic theory is also a myth. No one has seen an atom; our eyes aren't fast enough. We can see only effects and make educated guesses about their causes. Since Heisenberg (in 1932), no scientist would go to the wall for the Bohr model of pellet electrons. Sometimes the electron acts like a pellet, sometimes like a wave. But the theory and the model are good working symbol systems—myths: a theory that attempts to concretize something which is *there* but which we can't see.

Likewise, physical descriptions of God are myths, trying to explain a reality we can't see in terms of realities we can see. Since God exists in a dimension of reality independent of time and space, God has no beard like the Ancient of Days, no right hand to sit at, no genitals; God is not male. But for people who *equate* the inadequate symbol with the reality it attempts to embody, such realizations can cause tailspins.

The critical point is rarely made by teachers who even mention myth: atoms and God—and original sin, and the resurrection, and transubstantiation—are not myths; only *the way we talk about* atoms and God are myths.

A distinction even my two seminary professors did not make.

Furthermore, it surprises even adult Christians when one asserts that a story—even a made-up story—can tell the truth. They are shackled to the false notion that nonfiction tells the truth and fiction tells . . . something else. They presume that unless a story is *historically* true, it has no truth at all. On the contrary, although *The Catcher in the Rye* never happened, it still tells more truth about the pains of growing up than all the literal adolescent psychology books I've ever read.

The Prodigal Son and the Good Samaritan stories never happened either; Jesus made them up, *in order* to tell truths his listeners would have balked at accepting if he'd given his answer literally instead of *through* the story. The Magi may never have arrived in Jerusalem, but their story tells a truth: Jesus came not merely for the poor, uneducated, Jewish shepherds, but also for the rich, learned Gentiles as well. Even the legendary addition (which never appears in Matthew's Gospel) of the white, black, and yellow skins expands that truth even further.

All that seemed so ridiculously obvious to a seminary professor who had pored over Mercia Eliade and Joseph Campbell. Any educated person should know that. It was not so obvious to a thirty-year-old Ph.D. in physics. Then what of a high school sophomore?

And yet, fearsome as it is, how many teachers dump the Gospel according to Mark (because it's the shortest) even on high school freshmen, with no more preparation than, "Read it by Monday, and we'll discuss it"? I know at least one school that takes the Book of Revelation with sophomores. Why not dump *Lear* on them, or *The Four Quartets?* For the untrained reader, young or old, two thousand years from first-century Judaism, there are as many mystifying allusions, cultural presuppositions, and symbolic approximations in Matthew as there are in *Hamlet.* And yet we hold *Hamlet* off until senior year, and every page is faced with a rabbit warren of footnotes! Too much, too soon.

Raymond Brown puts it tersely in the *JBC* article on hermeneutics (71:15):

> Because scripture is inspired and presumably this inspiration is for the good of all, there has arisen the fallacy that everyone should be able to pick up the Bible and read it profitably. If this implies that everyone should be able to find out what the sacred author is saying, without preparation or study, it really demands of God in each instance a miraculous dispensation from the limitations imposed by difference of time and circumstances.

Every teacher has experienced the infuriatingly innocent ignorance this fallacy engenders: "My opinion is as good as anyone else's!" Or, when the student has read a verse for the first time and you've pored over it for a lifetime: "Well, that's *your* opinion," or "I can *read!*" It's easier to teach a foreign language than to teach Scripture. Because foreign languages begin with baby steps.

---

66 *Atoms and God . . . are not myths;* only *the way we talk about atoms and God are myths.* **99**

Baby Steps

Start with figures of speech. Don't presume students remember them from English class. They don't. Let them see how commonplace hyperbole and irony and allusion are in their everyday lives: "I'm gonna *kill* you for that! . . . Nice dress. Salvation Army? . . . Who the hell are you, Ann *Landers?*" Then show them that there's no reason to be troubled when Jesus pulls the same kind of jokes: "It's as easy for a rich man to get into heaven as for a camel to get through the eye of a needle. . . . Happy are those who mourn. . . . [John] is the Elijah who was to return."

Students themselves automatically explain things and people their listeners don't know by analogy to things and people they do know: "You never met Alfie? Well, he's a pig." Now, Alfie doesn't have a curly tail or whiskers or trotters, but the listeners have a better idea of him than they did before. Jesus did the same thing: "The Kingdom of God is like a banquet . . . a mustard seed . . . finding a treasure in your field."

The trouble is that none of the students I've ever taught had been shown how to de-compact a metaphor, just that it was "a comparison without *like* or *as.*" List all the things you can say about pigs that you can say about Alfie. Let's say you're boppin' along in your field and your foot hits something. "La," you exclaim, "my foot has struck something. It looks like a box." So you dig and dig and, lo, it *is* a box! And you crack open the lock, and creak open the lid and . . . it's *filled* with gold and rubies and diamonds! And it's all yours! I don't know about you, but the first thing I'd yell is "Holy [beep]!" Which goes to show that if you haven't shouted "Holy [beep]!" about being a Christian, you haven't found the Kingdom of God yet.

Young people's lives are also crowded with symbols: an athletic letter is just a piece of cloth, but somehow it's been made "holy" by a season of blood, sweat, and tears. The flag is also just a piece of cloth, but don't burn it near a construction site. A little kid leaning back against his dad's chest watching TV or a little girl with meticulously corn-rowed hair says "love" better than the forty-three lines in my dictionary defining love. Just so: look at a crucifix; it's *the* symbol that captures what Christianity means; it's a statue of a corpse. What does it tell you about what being Christian meant to the first Christian?

Since human life began, men and women have sat around campfires trying to understand their lives through stories. Every culture has had myths of creation and of the way to pass through the stages of life with dignity and honor. Fairy tales (see Bruno Bettelheim) are age-old stories that tell of becoming a physical and psychological adult, and they are as true today as they were thousands of years ago when they were first told. "Beauty and the Beast" never happened, and yet it tells a profound truth: anything ugly, once it is loved, becomes beautiful. "Cinderella" is the same story as the "Magnificat."

Even if some visitor from heaven could prove that Jesus' miracles were exaggerations dreamed up by the later Church to gussy up the message, what difference would it make? What truth is the miracle story trying to tell? Perhaps Peter never did get out of the boat and walk across the water to Jesus. That's not the point. The point is that once Peter forgot *himself*, his shortcomings, his limitations, and kept his eyes on Jesus, he could do what he had always thought was unthinkable! Perhaps the Big Fisherman never walked on water, but the Coward and Deserter of Good Friday died on a cross head down. That's a miracle.

Our audiences remain comfortably complacent in the face of a message that was calculated to upset, to provoke a total reversal of values: a conversion. There are many causes for that complacency, but I believe the root cause is that they have never really learned to read that message for themselves, without a teacher or a priest to explain it.

We keep giving them food for thought rather than, like the wise Mao, giving them a fishing pole and teaching them how to fish for themselves.

TWELVE

Mass and Teenagers

It's hardly news that more and more young people find something better to do with their Sunday mornings than go to Mass. Most parents of youngsters who still go can testify that it's usually a hassle and that, quite often, when the teenager goes away to college he or she leaves the Mass habit at home. Priests conducting pre-Cana conferences more and more frequently find that the couple's wedding Mass will be the first (and quite likely the last) in a long time. All of which proves that a large number of our young find the Mass neither meaningful, nor important, nor relevant to their lives. In their defense, I might add that, for many of their parents, membership in the Church is also as peripheral to their real lives as membership in the Kiwanis. Like the battles in Northern Ireland and in the Near East, family arguments about Mass usually have less to do with religion than they do with power.

Pastors and parents often lay the blame for this indifference too quickly and unfairly on the Catholic schools. Teachers in turn blame the diocesan clergy and parents—or TV or Madison Avenue or the bomb or God knows what. It's time we stopped trying to assign guilt, admit we have a common and quite serious problem, and start finding ways to alleviate it.

Parents suspect that when their child gives up religious practice, the child has lost faith in God. It's not that simple.

First, Mass attendance is an external act, and guessing another's motives for attending—or not—is just that: guessing. I have a difficult enough time assessing my own motives to be certain of others'. When we were seminarians, if we all stumbled down at six o'clock for morning visit, the rector could assure himself that we all went upstairs after it and dutifully put in our hour's meditation before Mass. Actually, we dutifully put ourselves back in bed for an hour. External practices are indicative, not probative, and the embers of belief in our young may be waiting for a bout with suffering, or marriage, or a child, or death to enliven them.

Second, I suspect a youngster's dropping Mass may not always indicate a loss of faith in God—for the simple reason that most young people have never actually made a real act of faith in God. Perhaps an act of faith in their parents' faith, or Sister's faith, or "Everybody believes in God," but not their own personal realization of and personal commitment to God.

In essence, we are asking our young to go to a weekly (and rather dull) testimonial dinner for a Person they have never really met and certainly feel no need for. We will never begin to solve the problem of Mass and teenagers until parents, priests, and religious educators all bow to the truth: that we are dealing with young people who are baptized but unconverted.

Here, I think, is the real answer: bringing youngsters to a personal relationship with God. All the religion courses and homilies in the world will remain as cold as calculus unless one has a commitment to the Person religion is all about. And that faith commitment is a calculated risk. The schools can supply the data, the calculation part, but the individual student is the only one who can supply the risk.

---

66 Family arguments about Mass usually have less to do with religion than they do with power. 99

It's surprising how many people fail to realize that. Their accusations seem to demand that religion classes either must have some magic formula to compel a "free" assent (which is a contradiction) or resort to the methods of Dickensian workhouses to get—if not true inner assent—at least less sulky attendance at Mass. Can't be done. Theology is what you know; religion is what you do. No one can teach religion. Only theology.

But just as adults judge young people's motives, young people do the same of adults' motives. If parents' attendance at Mass at least seems to be a perfunctory and joyless fulfillment of form, if God is never spoken of in the home as a Person with whom the parents have a real personal relationship, the child assumes that, even for the parents, the forty-five minutes on Sunday is at worst phony and at best deadened formalism. Perhaps the parent does pray daily, perhaps he or she does have a true relationship with God, but I wonder in how many homes a parent ever talks about it. Parents talk plentifully of their business and social relationships, but in my experience they rarely speak of their divine relationship. How many parents ever tell their children how they came to meet the living God? Unless that happens, religion for the young remains something unreal, to be endured a few classes a week and once on Sunday, until they get sprung.

Of course they are wrong. Of course they are evading the most meaningful relationship of their lives. But whipping a boy or girl to church is like forcing a boy to go to a prom with a homely neighbor. He'll go. But there won't be much communication and little likelihood of a personal relationship. And he's not likely to ask her out again.

Is that all parents want? If the son or daughter went to Mass without grousing, would they be satisfied and forget the whole thing? Is that all Catholicism means? That's the message the young are certainly getting.

I do believe that everyone has an obligation to worship God at least weekly—but not because the Church tells me, not because it's a mortal sin to miss, not because I'll go to hell. I don't go to Mass every week because the third commandment forces me to—any more than I visited my mother in the nursing home every week because the fourth commandment forced me to. I do both because an honest recognition of my place in the universe obliges me to. I go—even when I "get nothing out of it"—because I owe it to God and to my parents for what they've done for me.

The difference in the two motives is between the Law of the Hebrews, which was written on stone, and the Law of Christ, which is written in (some of) our hearts. Before, I went to Mass because the Church "forced" me to go; now, I go because *I* force me to go. The key, of course, is that I realize my indebtedness.

Young people take the gift of existence for granted, just as they take their mothers' labor pains for granted. It's never crossed their minds, nor do they ever grasp the truth that both existence and their mothers' labor pains were gifts they themselves did nothing to deserve. If they don't realize they've been given a gift, it's presumptuous to expect them to be grateful. And if they're not grateful to the mother they see every day, how can they be grateful to a God they're not too sure is even there?

If youngsters have never faced death or real want, if their complacency has never been seriously threatened, they have never faced their own finitude or dependence. Who needs God? And it follows with iron logic: Who needs Mass?

And It Gets Worse

Add to all this the confusion in the Church. Priests and nuns "leaping the league" became so commonplace that they don't even raise an eyebrow anymore. Yet these were the very people who counseled youth to chastity and the sanctity of one's obligations to the Church. What's more, any issue of *Time* or a diocesan paper shows that the professionals of the Church spend at least as much time laying ambushes for one another as for their common Enemy. "If the management is confused, don't invest."

Add also the very real (to the youngster) distinction between "Catholicism" and "Christianity." Catholicism consists exclusively in telling me the things I can't do; Christianity means doing nice little things for the neighbor once in a while, which makes Catholicism only a negative limit on my choices and Christianity little different from the Lions Club. Neither sounds worth getting up for any morning, much less the morning after party night and a celebration worthy of the word.

Even further, add the effect of Madison Avenue on a youngster's values. Add up all the hours priests, nuns, and parents have spoken about religious values and compare that to the countless hours TV, billboards, and movies have *demonstrated* material values, and the Church loses hands down. Every ad promises instant gratification or your money back. Young people expect the same of the Church. Sorry, Charlie. It can't deliver. You get what you give; that's the gospel in a nutshell.

All these factors in the disillusionment of the young are abetted by the fact that they realize their parents never read the Scriptures, that their actions prove they don't buy that jazz from Jesus about selling all and giving to the poor, laughing at competition, accepting who you are and what you have. I wonder how many Catholic parents even realize that the message of Jesus does run as counter to our American culture of consumerism as communism does.

---

66 *Theology is what you know; religion is what you do. No one can teach religion. Only theology.* **99**

By far the most lethal argument young people have against the Church and Mass is the manifest lack of joy in both Church and Mass. Like any potential convert (which is precisely what our young are), they look at the Church and say, "OK. If you've found the rock-bottom truth about human life, if you've really found the Good News that sets you free, why can't I *see* it in the way you act? You don't seem any more joyful or free or alive than Protestants, or Jews, or even atheists. The way you act shouts so loudly I can't hear what you preach." And there they have us.

The Church they live in bears so little resemblance to the ideal Church they hear of in religion class, small wonder that kids get the mixed-up idea that we want them to go to Mass only to keep up the attendance figures and the collections. They're wrong, of course. But that's not the problem. The problem is they think they're right and won't be convinced or converted by how we argue, but only by how we act.

What, Then, to Do?

As I said before, the concentration of religious education—in school, at home, in church—should focus on fostering a personal relationship between the teenager and God, particularly by elders honestly sharing with their young their own relationship with God. One ordinarily does not achieve a friendship with a person, divine or human, by having a debate about that person with a third party—although far too many religion classes and family discussions end up that way. One gets to know and love a person by acknowledging his or her presence, being with that person a lot, sharing. But how many parents or pastors or pedagogues talk openly to young people about their own prayer life: how to begin praying, how often they do it, what kinds of things they say, what it means to them? Why should youngsters try to know God better when they have no knowledge that their parents know God at all?

Making the God of the Textbooks real is not just one of the aims of religious education; it is *the* aim. All talk of the Church is mere historical curiosity; all talk of morality is mere ethical debate; all talk of liturgical innovation is merely realigning the lodge procedures—unless one has met and cares about God or at the very least feels grateful to God.

But meanwhile, while we're waiting for the Holy Spirit to arrive, we have to do something that will make the obligatory Mass more of a help for the unwilling teenager. At the very least, the Mass should not itself be an actual obstacle to finding God. Those of us with faith know that, no matter how slovenly the performance of the Mass, no matter how dull and meaningless the prayers, no matter how bored the priest, the Mass "works" *ex opere operato.* Consoling, but no justification for making it a test of the smoking flax and the bent reed.

Since the advent of English, much of the mystique and most of the poetry have been vacuumed out of the Mass. Thirty years ago even atheists could find themselves unwittingly drawn into the mystery through the cadences of the Latin or even the lusty, convinced belting of "Holy God, We Praise Thy Name." To them it could be as fascinating as an Oriental rite still is to us. Now, however, we have a Mass with such outlandish phrases as "our spiritual drink" and such tame literalism as "This is the Lamb of God," instead of the far stronger, "Behold! The Lamb of God." I'm by no means advocating a return to Latin, but let us have a Mass written by a poet rather than one that sounds written by a canon lawyer or a speculative theologian.

The answer is not merely to tack on a folk group or to turn the Mass into a rock concert, with the Mass part sneaked in (*ex opere operato*) while the kids aren't looking. Nor will kindly words from the pastor be enough to enliven the timid mooing back of "and with your spirit." Just as the call to Christianity itself, the call of our young to all priests and parish councils today is a call to genuine metanoia—a radical inner reversal.

The climate of the Mass is diametrically the opposite of the climate of a rock concert. One can sum up the cause in a single word: uptightness. People are afraid to respond heartily to the Mass, afraid to stand out. They are still shy and somewhat intimidated even by the greeting of peace; husbands and wives actually shake hands with one another! Yet the gospel claims to make us free, more willing to risk, and therefore more alive.

If some alien invader were to sneak into a parish Mass, would he or she be able to discern it was a celebration?

Practica Quaedam

The Priest.   Since the priest is, for the moment, the only one visibly participating in the Mass, the place to begin is with the celebrant. No matter how flaccid the prayers he's provided, he needn't say them like a zombie. I've preached at Masses where the "celebrant" read the prayers with all the deadening objectivity of a coroner. Obviously, no one in the parish was Christian enough to tell the man he was failing at his job.

---

66 *Making the God of the Textbooks real is not just one of the aims of religious education; it is* the aim. 99

The devil in me has sometimes prodded me to suggest that the bishops should command their subjects to register their approval or disapproval of the celebration by the degree of their offering in the collection basket. If I were ever made bishop (which is as likely as the Ayatollah naming me Shah of Iran), my first diocesan appointment would be a Mass reviewer for the diocesan paper, who would do for parish Masses what Gael Sheehey does for restaurants and Siskel and Ebert do for movies: make 'em or break 'em. I wouldn't be the first bishop assassinated.

Like every dramatic presentation, the Mass must have both its joyful and its solemn moments. What if the priest were to ad lib a bit puckishly now and again? If he takes himself too seriously, so will the congregation. If he himself is upright, self-defensive, insecure, the audience will respond in kind, and both priest and congregation will be a living denial of the gospel they preach and profess.

Saying Mass eight or ten times a week can make it become routine for the priest; but for the faithful, Sunday is the only time their lives and the life of the Church visibly intersect. And the priest's attitude is quite clear from his tone; many youngsters find it hard to believe that a priest who can rattle through the words of consecration with all the ardor of a conductor calling out station stops truly comprehends what is transpiring at his fingertips.

Homilies.   Of course, homilies must be relevant. But *relevant* surely doesn't mean inveighing against office parties the Sunday before Christmas and far less extolling the need for a new organ or carpeting. Rightly or wrongly, for the "barely convinced"—and that includes most of our young people—the homily is "the most important part of the Mass." Because they're hungry.

Young or old, rich or poor, the gut issues are the same: self-distaste, loneliness, the need to love, the need to overcome self-protectiveness in order to love in return. Perhaps few youngsters feel a gut need to worship once a week, but there's hardly a one who doesn't crave the reassurance that he or she is indeed worth loving.

Hymns.   In nearly every parish where I've ever said Mass, the hymns are pitched so high that they are accessible only to coloraturas and castrati. "They're all written in that key." Then transpose them. "I don't know how." Then hire someone.

And the hymns themselves are so bland and passive that it would be difficult to imagine Michael Jackson injecting any life into them. They all remind us that we shouldn't be afraid, that God cuddles us like the baby sheep we are and gives us rest. There are no clarion calls, no challenges, no exhortations to stand up and be counted. But a clarion call is precisely what the young have always hungered for!

In the unlikely event of my elevation to the purple, my second official act would be to begin a talent search—at no matter what cost—for musicians able to create music and lyrics that can move not just the lips but the heart.

The Format.   Some parishes have family Masses at which homilists are told to preach to the children. But I can't think of any audience that needs preaching less than children do. Meanwhile, their parents' spirits remain unchallenged, and the adolescents in the family spend the Mass playing pornographic movies on the insides of their corneas. Other parishes have a far better system: three different Liturgies of the Word in three different locations: one for children, one for teenagers, one for adults. It takes a bit of time, but the sole purpose of our gathering on Sunday is not to see how quickly we can clear out the parking lot.

Any teacher, any homilist, any prophet is a salesperson. It doesn't make any difference if he or she has the most perfect product in the world—if the audience is completely indifferent both to the product and to the pitch. When that's the case, the serious salesperson goes back and reworks the pitch. It is time, I think, for the American Church and for each individual priest to stop presuming the interest of their audience, particularly of their young audience. It's a buyers' market, and our young simply aren't eager to buy.

It makes no sense to say the young shouldn't be that way; they are that way, and it's our mission to reach them where they are: spoiled, complacent, unappreciative. But at the same time, they are also just as confused as every adolescent has been since the days of Socrates and before: they yearn to know who they are, where they fit in; no single one of them does not long to be a somebody, to rise to a challenge, to make a difference. We have the answer to those needs, if only we can find a language and a liturgy that can communicate that answer to that audience.

When Matteo Ricci went to China, the silk-robed mandarins he sought to convert were indifferent to the gospel, simply because nothing of substance could be learned from a round-eyed foreigner got up in a tatty black cassock. So, Matteo Ricci clad himself in silk, his vow of poverty notwithstanding. And the mandarins began to listen. The missionaries to Malabar adapted the Mass to the language, customs, and understanding of the people to whom they were sent. And the people of Malabar began to listen. But the official Church put a halt to that. The people of Malabar would simply have to adapt themselves to European ways. And the people of Malabar stopped listening.

---

66 *If some alien invader were to sneak into a parish Mass, would he or she be able to discern it was a celebration?* **99**

I fear we are doing the same thing today with our young. And I fear it is having exactly the same results. The wise Pogo was right: "We have met the enemy, and he is us."

PART THREE

Relationships with Others

THIRTEEN

The Roots of Evil

Joyce was right. Truth pops out from the most unexpected places. My best definition of evil came from Dr. Scott Peck's eight-year-old son: "Daddy, evil is 'live' spelled backwards."

Evil is anything radically opposed to life. If the specific difference of human life over animal life is that we can know, and love, and grow in our ability to know and love, then evil is anything that de-grades us—makes us less able to know, and love, and grow. Evil is killing—not just the body, but the self, the spirit, the soul.

Youngsters are willing to accept that there is evil, but it's "out there": war, exploitation, drugs. I find it difficult to convince them that they are themselves capable of increasing the flood of evil, perhaps not in dramatic ways but surely evil. Especially with kids brought up on Jesus, the Warm Fuzzy, it's no easy task to make them accept that casual character assassination may seem petty but negates a human being, that shunning ugly kids or unathletic kids or pimply kids is the same kind of bigotry as the Klan's and Archie Bunker's. Petty evil is still evil. We're in the same business as the Mob, except the Mob has a broader perspective and more guts.

There are really two broad brands of evil. Physical evil is truly destructive of life—tornadoes, cancer, drought, death itself. But physical evil occurs most often through no human fault. It is something we have to lay at the feet of God, and defending God against the endless litany of "Why-would-a-good-God" charges is an enormous and painful task, one that will have to wait for another time.

---

66 Evil is killing—not just the body, but the self, the spirit, the soul. 99

Moral evil, on the other hand, is a willful human invention—rape, war, genocide, all manners of human inhumanity. Human wickedness is in no way blameable on God—except that, for reasons unknown to us, God bestowed the gift of freedom on a tribe of inadequately evolved apes. So the question of moral evil is not "Why would a good God," but why would human beings degrade one another—and themselves—to the level of beasts, or vegetables, or stepping-stones?

The answers to that question—at least the most common in Western thought—are pretty well covered by four novels familiar even to most high school readers: *The Exorcist, Lord of the Flies, The Catcher in the Rye,* and *The Lord of the Rings.*

The Exorcist posits a prehuman source of evil, a disembodied intelligence radically inimical to the human spirit: Lucifer, the Father of Lies, a malevolent entity able to seduce but never to coerce. It plays on our weakness, our restlessness with creaturehood, our need to be Number One. Taken literally, the Book of Genesis seems to say the same, and the exorcisms of the New Testament seem to give credence to its existence.

Lord of the Flies sees no need to blame our wickedness on anyone else outside our savage selves—though most of our lives are spent trying to scapegoat our guilt away onto some demon, or beast, or pig's head on a stick. It is only the thin and very fragile veneer of civilization imposed on us that keeps the beast within us in check. Voltaire would agree that we are evolving ever so slowly from brutishness to politeness. It's a position on human weakness shared by Karl Marx and B. F. Skinner: uproot freedom or ride herd on it, and we will have peace.

Even though students tell me that *The Catcher in the Rye* and *Lord of the Flies* both "tell it like it is," *Catcher* says precisely the opposite of *Lord of the Flies*. Far from being savages from the womb, we are all born as innocent as Holden's sister, Phoebe, and it is our forced immersion into so-called civilization—adults and business and phonies—that corrupts us. Rousseau would agree: we are Tarzan and Jane perverted by our socialization. It is a position most of the Flower Children of the sixties shared.

The Lord of the Rings rests on the premise that there may quite possibly be an alien force of evil outside us which antedated the human will—or at least there are human hosts who have totally surrendered to evil. Evil has no power over us without our cooperation, just as God has no power over us without our cooperation. But Tolkien's trilogy also makes a far more subtle point: not to resist evil actively *is* to cooperate with it. And in Gollum, I think one finds a far more potent amd fearsome embodiment of human corruption than in Milton's Lucifer or Goethe's Mephistopheles. Gollum is the inversion of human life, a self-contained darkness.

Satan

In the Hebrew Scriptures, where Satan makes only
rare appearances, as in the Book of Job, Satan is not
pictured as God's enemy. Rather, the word *satan* originally
meant only "adversary," in the sense of two friends
playing a game. Since human beings can't grow without
rising to challenge, God sent Lucifer, the chief of the
archangels, to play the adversary, to test humans just as
teachers test children in order to make them grow. But
in the cloud of legends that grew in Judeo-Christian
culture—perhaps under the influence of Zoroastrianism,
which postulated a good God of light opposed by an evil
god of darkness—the separation between God and Lucifer
became permanent and unbridgeable.

According to the legend (which never appears in
Scripture), Lucifer was God's beautiful chief of staff and
his principal teacher: the Light-Bearer. But as time went
on, Lucifer fell in love with his task—or more precisely:
with himself—relishing his cleverness and power far more
than he relished God. Meanwhile, for century on century,
God and Lucifer had failed to lure humanity freely to
evolve away from savagery and toward knowing and
loving, so God decided to give an example of the fully
evolved human he had intended all along: his Son, who
was the Good News, living truth and love, the ultimate
goal of evolution.

Ah, but that was a humiliating displacement of
Lucifer. No longer was he the darling, the second, the
principal teacher for God. In a burst of primal arrogance,
Lucifer refused to bow to the truth—which *is* the will of
God. And so, Lucifer plummeted from heaven into
darkness, where he lurks, corroding with dreams of
revenge—against God, against Christ, and against all
humankind over whom he was once archmessenger.
Milton captured it perfectly in Lucifer's defiant cry:
"Better to reign in hell than serve in heaven." It is a cry
echoed by Adam: "I will become like God." The cry of
Oedipus: "I can outwit the gods." The cry of Faust, and

Raskolnikov, and, in our own tiny and less dramatic ways, it is the cry of each of us: Who needs God?

Had you asked me twenty years ago if I believed in an intelligent, disembodied force of evil, I'd most likely have snorted, "Tommyrot! (Or something less genteel.) This *isn't* the thirteenth century. One *does* have advanced de*grees.*" But I was suddenly vaulted up there onto the big ol' silver screen in a pornographic horror film, and I was asked to give talks all around the country (at obscenely inflated stipends) about "What's a Nice Priest Like You Doing in a Movie Like That?" So I had to find out why I had loaned my name and presence to such a venture, other than for a sinfully enjoyable ego trip.

❝ *Not to resist evil actively* is to *cooperate with it.* ❞

The first fact to grasp is that everything which occurs in *The Exorcist*—except for the reverse English and the head turning completely around—has actually occurred many, many times: levitation, moving objects without touching them, speaking languages the victim has never learned—the lot. The question is not whether such phenomena occur; that is a given. The question is what *causes* them. It's true that we use only about 10 percent of our mental powers, but to assert out of hand that such phenomena *must* be caused by some unknown gizmo in the brain is as gratuitous as asserting that they must be caused by some disembodied force of evil. Sez who? Both are pontifications without evidence or argument.

Carl Sagan says in *Cosmos* that, by the law of probability, there are alien intelligences on at least one hundred planets in the universe. On the contrary, however, he—with many, many others—flatly denies even the possibility of any transcendent, otherworldly entities whatever—not only Satan, but God and an afterlife as well. That seems just as close-minded and unscientific as the Church's denial of Galileo's sun-centered solar system. To deny that any entity *can* exist is as arrogant as denying that curved space, black holes, and parallel universes can exist.

When one goes to a funeral home and says to the bereaved, "Ah, she's in a better life now," the speaker is perhaps unaware of that statement's astonishing corollaries. If one admits an afterlife (even if only in moments of helplessness), he or she admits persons actually survive death, that reality is not limited to the palpable, that beings exist free of the limits of time and space, that there is a dimension to human life impervious to the scientific method. "There are more things in heaven and on earth, Horatio, than are dreamt of in your philosophy."

And, demonstrably, not all the people who have died were good. Once you've accepted the existence of God—and a transcendent dimension to reality—you've opened the door to at least the possibility of a wicked disembodied intelligence: to Satan.

I don't know whether Satan exists. Dr. M. Scott Peck, who is a psychiatrist, was invited twice to be on teams involved in exorcisms, and although he was a confirmed skeptic at first, he ended up a firm believer in Satan. In *People of the Lie,* he describes the two cases. "As a hard-headed scientist," he says, "which I assume myself to be, I can explain 95 percent of what went on in those two cases by traditional psychiatric dynamics. . . . I could talk in terms of brainwashing, deprogramming, reprogram-ming, catharsis, marathon group therapy and identifi-cation. But I am left with a critical 5 percent I cannot explain in such ways. I am left with the supernatural—or better yet, the subnatural. . . . The end of each exorcism proper was signaled by the departure of this Presence from the patient and the room."

If Lucifer does in fact exist, however, Peck makes some points that are well worth underlining—lest we all go off half-cocked in terror. First, "possession is no accident." It results from a gradual process of selling out, and in both cases he studied, there was a significant emotional problem before the possession occurred. Also, in the majority of cases the victim had had involvement with the occult, often beginning with something as apparently innocent as a Ouija board. (This is a reason I include this chapter: evil is *fascinating,* and the media make dabbling in the occult at least as intriguing as trying grass.)

Again, I don't know whether what sometimes occurs when dallying with the occult is caused by some sub-natural power or autosuggestion or by some other power of which we know nothing. But I do know from two cases I've been involved in peripherally that bad things— inexplicable things—*do* happen. I'd advise anyone to stay away from them, just as I'd advise anyone not to play around nuclear waste dumps. I know as little about evil as I know about radiation, but what I do know of both is unrelievedly bad.

Just as someone who fools around with marijuana isn't necessarily going on to crack or heroin, someone who fools around with a Ouija board isn't necessarily going to end up like the heroine of *The Exorcist.* But it's an innocent first step toward it.

Finally, if the cause of possession is indeed demonic, the demon has no power without cooperative acceptance of its lies, just as TV has no power without cooperative acceptance of its lies. And the demon has no power *outside* a human host. It can threaten violence or death, but it is helpless without the cooperation of its host. Its principal weapon is fear, and its archenemy is confidence within anyone who confronts it. But evil—whether demonic or human—is surprisingly obedient to authority, but not mere delegated authority, *moral* authority. Even if *The Exorcist* were merely a parable of evil, the figure of Father Merrin is the answer to fear of evil: confidence, not in oneself but in the One in whom you have placed your trust. The root of the word *confidence* is, after all, *fides:* faith.

To put it in a simple way: if you are ever confronted with what you believe to be truly evil, you have a big Brother who can beat up Satan any time he wants. Not the best of motives for a personal relationship with Christ, but a motive nonetheless.

Socialization

The other three novels' answers to the question of human wickedness come down to a matter of good and bad socialization: upbringing, the influences of outside forces on one's freedom. Both *Lord of the Flies* and *The Catcher in the Rye* contradict one another, and yet something tells the students I've taught that they are both true. There is in fact something beastly and difficult to govern in us—what Freud calls the id. But it can be not only governed but utilized if it is civilized, by what Freud calls the superego and ego. Like fire, the id is a source of power, but only if it is controlled. Unchecked, it becomes a savage beast.

Animals cannot be evil; they do only what their instincts dictate. But humans have very few inborn instincts—one is the sex drive and another is the drive for self-preservation. But we are not even prisoners of those two instincts; we can go counter to them by vows of celibacy in order to serve a higher cause or by sacrificing our lives even for our enemies. Animal nature is a command; human nature is an invitation we are free to turn down. And right there—in our freedom to resist the invitation to evolve as human—is the taproot of human wickedness. Refusing to be content with the truth, with things as they really are, we yearn to upgrade ourselves to be God—perfect, the center of all reality, arbiters of what can be true—but in every case, trying to outreach our capacity, we end up degrading ourselves to brute beasts.

> **❝ Right there—in our freedom to resist the invitation to evolve as human—is the taproot of human wickedness. ❞**

Let me look first at a simple—even trivial—case of human evil: myself as a child, and then show the opposite, abysmal extreme of evil, when self-centeredness becomes a way of life: Gollum. We all find ourselves in between those two extremes: slightly soiled innocence and utter depravity. The only real question that faces us is which direction our lives are heading: downward toward the darkness, or upward toward the light.

When I was about seven or eight, some friends and I were playing in the street when an old codger came out and bawled us out. We were kids, unaware of anyone else in the galaxy except ourselves, so we had no idea we were disturbing him, or that his wife might be inside dying of cancer. But we plotted revenge. In a field we found a dead rat, and I was deputed to hurl the noxious rodent onto the old man's porch. Every nerve trembling, I crept up to the house, hurled it, and ran.

That evening, the phone rang and my dad picked it up. "No," I heard him say, "I don't think Bill would do something like that." But he came over and asked if I'd thrown the rat on Mr. So-and-So's porch. And I said, "No." And my dad believed me. Well, I was plunged into torment. My dad had never done anything unkind to me; he'd never lied to me; and I'd lied to him. So I went out into the garage, picked up a nail, and scratched in the wall, "I get blamed for things I didn't do."

There I was, not more than four feet tall, and already an enemy to the truth—because the truth was insupportable. I couldn't bear living with the truth; so— omnipotently—I changed the truth to something I could live with.

As I said, a trivial case. But when that kind of evasion of truth becomes a way of life, what it turns you into is Gollum.

Gollum had murdered in order to possess the Ring of Power—just as Adam and Eve had disobeyed in order to possess the knowledge of good and evil, equality with God. From that moment on, Gollum lived encaved in darkness, afraid of the watchful sun. He felt misunderstood and ill-used by everyone, so he spent his days telling himself self-justifying stories till he almost believed them, and his life became a matrix of lies. As Gandalf says, "He was altogether wretched. He hated the dark, and he hated light more: he hated everything, and the Ring most of all. . . . He hated it and loved it, as he hated and loved himself. He could not get rid of it. He had no will left in the matter." Gollum became devoured by the Ring of Power.

I said before that what specifies our nature in contrast to animal nature is that we can know and love, as God does, and what specifies our nature in contrast to God's nature is that we are imperfect: we are invited to grow as knowers and lovers. Our nature is to reach upward and outward, but in order for that to happen, we must be humble before the immutable truth, we must be vulnerable to other people. Ah, there's the rub.

Humankind is an uneasy fusion of angel and beast. The fallen angel in us draws us upward to narcissism, and the beast in us draws us downward toward inertia. Those

are the two taproots of human evil: narcissism and inertia.
No need of Satan.

Narcissism is arrogance, the conviction one is, in fact,
the only person of importance. It is not healthy pride
in a job well done; it is perfectionism, the pretension to
godlikeness, with the inevitable concomitant terror that
one might be wrong: NOT-OK. But since, by the nature
of things, we are not God, and we can see reality only
imperfectly, we are bound to be wrong—or mistaken, or
off-the-mark, or guilty at least some of the time. Narcissism is the refusal to make peace with that humbling
truth. As C. S. Lewis says, the Enemy of Human Nature
needn't turn us into archfiends; it needs merely to hand
us a mirror. That way we are immobilized; there is no one
to know or love (or even hate) but oneself.

Inertia is the law of matter: any body at rest will
remain at rest unless moved by another force—like the
human will. Thus, we have little taste for the work of
gathering data, sifting the truth from the garbage, living
with tentative conclusions. We want it all: the Ring of
Power, the fruit of the tree of knowledge—the quick,
painless grasp of certitude.

So we withdraw inward, shut down our borders, and
become aggressively defensive against any intrusions by
unpleasant truths: for instance, that although all of us are
important, none of us is essential; that just as surely as
fire burns and objects fall, when I rape or starve or murder
or lie to another human being, I de-grade both him or her
and myself. No matter what I do, I find a justification for
it. I am OK; I have nothing to apologize for, nothing to
confess.

Were you ever in an argument—especially with your
parents—when suddenly the light flashed and you
realized, "My God. They're right!"—and you kept on
arguing anyway, even after you knew you were wrong?
That's the taproot of evil: not genuine pride, not money:
narcissism.

159

Eric Fromm puts it: "The more they continue to make wrong decisions, the more the heart hardens. . . . With each step along the wrong road, it becomes increasingly difficult for them to admit they *are* on the wrong road, often only because they have to admit that they must go back to the first wrong turn, and must accept the fact that they have wasted energy and time." Sound familiar?

---

66 *Those are the two taproots of human evil: narcissism and inertia.* 99

Because persons self-victimized by narcissism and inertia refuse to take in information contrary to their desires, their attitudes harden. They move further and further away from the light. As Dr. Peck writes, "If someone criticizes an attitude of mine, I feel he or she is criticizing *me.* If one of my opinions is proved wrong, then *I* have been proved wrong. My self-image of perfection has been shattered."

Such people live autistic lives in which there are no other persons: literally in a world of their own. Without the salvific gift of legitimate guilt, they refuse to blame themselves even for harm they are genuinely responsible for. They scapegoat, projecting their guilt on others: their parents, their jobs, the economy, the government, the "System." Their primary occupation is disguise, not only from others but even more importantly from themselves. Their lies—just like the Ouija board—begin innocently enough, but they quickly become an escalating series of compromises with dishonesty. And the one thing that could heal them is the one thing they most fear: honest confrontation of the truth about life and about themselves. They are utterly wretched, but as Milton's Lucifer cries,

"Better to reign in hell than serve in heaven," better to be king, no matter how cramped and airless the kingdom, than to live with the uncertainty and doubt that are the undeniable concomitants of being human.

Evil—enslavement to narcissism and inertia—is not limited to individuals. This ignorant omnipotence infects groups as well, since groups are merely a multiplicity of individuals: the in-crowds, the cliques, the gangs; the Hatfields and the McCoys; lobbies, special interests, corporations, churches, nations. "We're all right. It's all those Jews, and slopes, and liberals, and conservatives, and Commies who are all wrong." We need no Satan to trigger our My Lais, our Holocausts, our Three-Mile Islands, Watergates, Contra scandals, ecological crimes. All we need is what, in our passion for self-justification, we call "enlightened self-interest."

What's more, the larger our institutions grow, the more segmented one level is from another, the more soulless they become, insulated minds and insulated consciences. "Decisions like that are above my pay grade. . . . Don't point the finger at me, I only load the bombs. . . . I was only following orders. . . . Don't blame me, blame the President. Blame the System. Blame my socialization."

And we arrive at the trouble-free sterility of *1984,* a society of Gollums.

Curing Evil

The cure for evil is rarely, if ever, literal exorcism. If the taproots of evil are narcissism and inertia, then the only cure for them is their opposites: humility and effort. If the principal occupations of evil people are disguise and erecting self-defenses, then the only cure is their opposite: honesty and vulnerability. If, as Dr. Peck says, evil people are "People of the Lie," then the only cure for them is the opposite: fearlessly confronting the truth.

Although it may sound ludicrously simple, I believe there are two weapons against evil far more powerful than holy water and incantations: confession and learning.

People are uncomfortable with confession. We always have been, but more so today, when we live in mortal terror of guilt trips. It's too upsetting to sit down every three or four months and assess, honestly, where we've taken those wrong turns. Far better to wile away the time with the *National Enquirer,* exulting at the motes in everyone else's eyes and never noticing the logs in our own eyes. After all, guilt is so . . . well, inhibiting. But what you get without guilt is My Lai. What you get without guilt is Auschwitz. What you get without guilt is Gollum: narcissism impregnable against humility or truth.

People are also uncomfortable with learning. Oh, for a few years the threat of failure, the whip of the SATs and GREs, the witless conviction that one needs a degree in order to make a decent living are enough to overcome inertia—at least at exam time. But when the gauntlet is over, when the whips and threats are stowed away, how many people ever read a book on their own? How many are content to pick their attitudes and opinions—and consequently their behavior—"off the rack," from the media, from the demagogues, from their pals down at Archie Bunker's bar?

Labrador retrievers wag their tails like crazy, even when they're ready to drop with exhaustion from chasing sticks—because that's what they were born to do. Human beings can know joy—which is the diametric opposite of evil—only when they, too, do what they were born to do: know and love and grow. But that can't happen unless one is humble before the truth, vulnerable to other people, dissatisfied with the old ways.

Oh, it costs. Unlike narcissism and inertia, knowing and loving and growing are not "givens"; they are invitations. To know and love and grow takes risk—the risk of leaving behind the comfortable in order to find something that may or may not be better, the risk of failure, the risk of being wrong, the risk of mockery from all the Gollums. But the alternative is, at least to some degree, evil—which is the opposite of "live."

---

66 *If the taproots of evil are narcissism and inertia, then the only cure for them is their opposites: humility and effort.* **99**

The primeval Christian symbols for evil and goodness are Adam and Jesus, the new Adam. Adam succumbed to the temptation to which we have all succumbed: eat this and you will become like God. But Christ—who *was* God—"did not cling to his equality with God, but instead he emptied himself [he gave it all up] to assume the condition of a slave and became as men are." And he went even further: he died horribly, and his penultimate words were words of doubt: "My God, my God, why have you abandoned me?" But his ultimate words were words of humility and trust: "But into your hands I commend my spirit." It is Jesus, vulnerable to the point of impotence, who is God's weapon against evil.

FOURTEEN

Good Guilt/ Bad Guilt

Poor old Mister Guilt. God's hit man. With only a few brief lapses over the centuries, he ruled the roost: kept the kids in line, held down the statistics on divorces and abortions and unwed motherhood, delivered a gratifying crop of confessions and vocations and conscience money each year, gave a certain disproportionate zest to our minor peccadillos, and provided the motivation for every detective story from *Oedipus* through *Macbeth* to *All the President's Men.* What would James Joyce or Woody Allen ever have written without old Mister Guilt?

But, truth to tell, he did get out of hand now and again. He'd often demand exorbitantly higher wages. He invented and quite successfully marketed some pretty paralyzing games: Scrupulosity, Hypersensitivity, Pharisaism, Neuroses, and How Far Can I Go. He hired an unsavory class of henchmen—Torquemada, Governor Danforth, Senator Joseph McCarthy, to name but a few. So, with the help of such odd bedfellows as Sigmund Freud and Hugh Hefner, biblical and liturgical reform, the pill, and the First Amendment, we drove Guilt from our tents in leprous disrepute, out there somewhere in the hinterlands between Salem, Massachusetts, and Las Vegas, Nevada.

Too bad, really. Because what we get without guilt is Auschwitz.

Don't get me wrong. I don't lament those dear-dead-days-beyond-recall when I wondered if I'd swallowed toothpaste after midnight and broken my Eucharistic fast. I don't hanker to get back to the days of "the Church taught" and "the Church teaching," where the one had nothing to say, and the other had nothing to learn. But I do chafe in a Church that's gone from iron-fisted to limp-wristed, from the arcane to the inane.

We're double-minded. On the one hand, we don't like anybody telling us what to do; we want flexibility, elbowroom, freedom—all the things, rightly or wrongly, we associate with Vatican II. On the other hand, we don't want to be confused; we want security, a road map, certitude—all the things, rightly or wrongly, we associate with Vatican I. There's only one problem with that: those two contrary desires in us have to make compromises with one another. Just as we can't have the majesty of pipe organs *and* the hominess of guitars both at once, we can't have freedom and certitude both at once.

Something unredeemed in us wants things simple and clear-cut, even when the reality is in no way simple or clear-cut. That something in us yearns irrationally for the good old days when a sin was either definitively deadly or utterly trivial, anything not forbidden was compulsory, and anything not compulsory was forbidden, and so many wonderful games could be played in class with "but what if" and "at what instant does unsullied innocence hit the greasy chute into the 'Mortal' bin?"

But, since Vatican II, a lot of the old rules have, it seems, disappeared—an absence that was supposed to make us all feel freer, more adult, able to decide for ourselves, unshackled from the anguish of needless guilt.

There are, it seems, no more dogmatic road maps to a clear conscience. We have, it seems, to find our own way, with no other compass than our "gut feelings."

As a result, we've traded guilt for anxiety.

A hundred years ago, Dostoevsky said that there is no gift a person will sooner surrender than freedom. And I don't believe we've really evolved so far in a hundred years that that's no longer true. The reason is that, in order truly to be free, one has to think for his or her self—which takes both effort and risk. Without the iron maidens of dogmatism, we have no hope of certitude that what we're doing is right or wrong. The best we can settle for is probability.

But I like to know where I stand and I don't like standing on a tightrope. I'm uncomfortable seated at a dinner party between Carrie Nation and Mae West. I'd prefer either a prayer meeting or an orgy. At least I'd know what's expected; at least I'd know what to wear.

One of the reasons that the bishops' recent calls to think—and act—for ourselves are not eagerly awaited is that we seem to be at the uttermost reach of a mood swing in history. What makes us so uneasy about the bishops' two most recent letters is that they're so *non*dogmatic. It doesn't matter what the dogma is, really, so long as it removes the burden of freedom, the burden of thinking things through for ourselves. Just so long as some Grand Inquisitor will take into his belly the griping cramps of our uncertainty and guilt.

Guilt can be a very healthy response. When I violate my values, guilt is the quite salutary and natural hunger that I set things right again.

Guilt is a very human and humanizing element in our lives; it makes us grow—often at times when we believed we had no more growing to do. But, like any good thing—humility, self-reliance, love—without the control of perspective and common sense, guilt can have the opposite effect from the one its Inventor intended. On the one hand, it can make us run in terror, dragging our smoke screens behind us. On the other hand, it can desensitize, dehumanize, leave us with rubbery spines. Like any other volatile emotion, guilt makes a very fine servant, but a wretched master.

Guilt—unless it metamorphoses into responsibility—cripples its host either into cowardice or callousness: gutless or heartless.

> **66** *Guilt is a very human and humanizing element in our lives; it makes us grow.* **99**

Too much guilt can lead us to hypersensitivity, scrupulosity, paralysis—as it has always done when the Puritan called the shots. Too little guilt can leave us nerveless, thick-skinned, unscrupulous, grabby—as it has always done when the Libertine owns the propaganda systems. Either way, a natural hunger, intended to make us humble before the truth of our need to grow, can be diverted into its precise opposite: narcissism. It matters little which brand—the scrupulous or the unscrupulous, just so long as it keeps us focused on *our* rights to be left alone.

Our days are filled with guilt signals, some trivial, some serious; some quite sensible, some quite stupid. On the one hand, "We lost that game because I didn't give more than 100 percent" can weigh far more heavily on the soul than "I cheated my parents out of their tuition money again today." On the other hand, one's horizons can be cracked open onto a far more realistic perspective when one realizes that "I negated a human person today" is far more needful of concern than "I had a few heart-stopping moments with *Penthouse* today."

There are only three real responses to guilt that I know of: at the one extreme, there is paralyzing anguish; at the other extreme, there is labotomizing suppression; and at the precarious balancing point between the two is acceptance.

The Tyranny of Guilt

Paralyzing anguish—scrupulosity—is the result of what Michael Cavanaugh calls "ambush theology"—God as Santa Claus. "He's makin' a list; he's checkin' it twice (at least); so you better watch out, baby!"

At least in my experience over the last decade, that's not really the greater of the problems—although there are, sadly, still people who spend too much time looking over their shoulders for the Fiery-Eyed Jehovah who invented hell. At that scrupulous end of the spectrum, I usually find superbly well-intentioned people who are victims of the Liberal Guilt Complex. They're not troubled any more that they had a soup on Friday that might have been made from beef stock. What ravages them is that they haven't done anything for those tragic children in Ethiopia. And the illiterate. And the homosexuals. And the bag ladies. And the ghettos. And the prisons. The list, of course, is endless.

Perversely, that corrosive guilt always finds a home in terribly generous people. Equally perversely, it's a generosity that is a first cousin to narcissism, to Oedipal self-sufficiency—in fact, to blasphemy. They have taken on a task that Jesus Christ himself was unable to perform. And they hate themselves for being unable to do what he failed to do: wipe out all the self-centeredness, exploitation, and hypocrisy—even in one small backwater province of the Roman Empire. At its worst, it either leaves the poor, generous-hearted victims wringing their hands in front of so many needy doorways, unable to decide which to help first, and thus helping none—or it lifts them onto white horses every morning and sends them charging off in all directions at once, getting in everyone's way, and often alienating even the very people they were trying to help.

If only the victims of this overblown guilt could sacrifice their claims to messianism, if only their generosity and enthusiasm were tempered with just a touch of perspective, and humor, and common sense, they could choose one doorway and do some good.

But I would rather argue the mission of the Christian apostle with Madalyn Murray O'Hair any day than with a social activist. I would also question the wisdom of raising up such an intense awareness of—and guilt for—global inhumanity in the young. Without offering some concrete means to assuage and expunge that guilt (in order to turn it into practical responsibility), such consciousness-raising, on the part of unquestionably well-motivated teachers, is pernicious.

The Abdication of Guilt

At the opposite extreme, there are the sociopaths: the guards at Buchenwald, the terrorists, the Mob hit men, the nonaddicted pushers, the men and women and even children in our own cities who can murder, rape, burn, and pillage without the slightest qualm of guilt. Some of them, according to experts, seem psychologically incapable of empathy or of a realization that their victims are equally persons, almost as if the moral circuits of their minds had never been connected. Others seem to have had whatever moral sense they may once have had cauterized by rage and smothered by hopelessness.

However, it's doubtful that any reader of these pages is among those tragic souls at the unscrupulous end of the moral spectrum. Most of us can persist along an immoral

path only if we somehow justify our action either by
twisting the truth out of shape, by forcing the end to
justify the means, or by merely letting time and habit
deaden that particular area of one's moral susceptibility.
Thus, the British and Argentines could convince themselves that the Falkland Islands were worth the death of
even one soldier—and along with him his unborn children
and their children. People can smoke grass, claiming it
hurts no one else and shutting from their minds the fact
that their marijuana money enables the Mob to hook
others on heroin and lure them into prostitution. In
Central America, better a malevolent Fascist than a
benevolent Communist.

Healthy Guilt

Guilt is wholesome only when it makes us change,
grow, take charge of our own actions in the future—so
that nobody else has to step in and take charge of them
for us. Guilt is good only when it is used—and left behind.

---

66 *Guilt is wholesome only when it
makes us . . . take charge of our own
actions in the future.* **99**

Becoming a grown-up happens without our consent.
One day we were children; the next day we were capable
of begetting children. On the contrary, adulthood comes
only at the price of very great struggle, humility—and at
times even humiliation—freely if painfully accepted.
The dividing line between childhood and adulthood is
acceptance of responsibility for who one is, what one does,
what one says. It's a responsibility to the truth, to the way

things and human beings are made. An adult demands to be accountable. Because if I'm not accountable, I'm negligible.

For the adult, there is no recourse to the old dodges: projection ("How else could I act after being socialized as I was?"), rationalization ("Everybody else does it and gets away with it"), denial ("That kind of reactionary thinking went out with the hoopskirt!"), displacement ("It wasn't really fornication; more like mutual masturbation"), euphemism ("Our pacification team leveled everything in the village to save it from the enemy").

As Thomas Aquinas said, "The sinner does not love himself too much; he does not love himself enough." Otherwise, sinners couldn't demean themselves so readily or, having demeaned themselves, allow themselves either to wallow in guilt or flee from it. Healthy adults have too much respect for themselves not to acknowledge the guilt, judge its extent, and atone.

Bad people don't go to confession. Only good people do. But it's pretty clear that far fewer people are going to confession than ever before.

Why? Part of the reason is healthy. We have shed the masochistic pleasures of nitpicking ourselves. But part also, I think, is unhealthy. Many of the fumbling *sequelae* to Vatican II have taken a great deal of the steel from our spines. The God of Job has been completely eclipsed by the Good Shepherd, who has to forgive anything, even if one isn't sorry.

Thank God we've left behind the blazing ire of God and the eternal *auto-da-fé* as a motivation for acknowledging the truth. But how does one sell spinelessness to the young? If the challenges of the gospel—not only to social change but to moral self-honesty—do not unnerve them in the slightest, have we really preached the gospel to them? Say what you will about Jerry Falwell and his colleagues. For my tastes, they are too simplistic, self-righteous, univocal. But they are also offering something that both the young and the not-so-young are quite naturally and normally hungry for: spine.

In our reading—and our teaching—of the gospel, I wonder if it isn't time to go back and sift out the passages where we do not find Jesus meek and mild: where he rails at the Pharisaic clergy of his religion, where he snarls "you devil!" at Peter, where he holds an uneasy rein on his temper when his first twelve seminarians whine, "What's in this for us?" and "I, uh, seem to recall your saying something about . . . thrones?"

❝ Healthy adults have too much respect for themselves not to acknowledge the guilt, judge its extent, and atone. ❞

Peter, the model disciple, is a perfect example to all of us who might feel a slight twinge that we're klutzing our call as disciples. He could hardly have missed the point more often. He flung his boasts to the heavens. But when it came to the crunch, he ran with all the others. And yet, what was it that drove him, all alone, to leave the locked upper room and go to the court of the high priest "to see the end"? Guilt? Loyalty to his friend despite his fear?

Even then, at the moment of his testing, Peter crumpled. He denied his friend and his Lord—not to a soldier with a knife at his throat. To a waitress. And not once. Three times. But when he realized what he had done, when his eyes were opened to the truth—to his guilt—"he went out and wept, and wept."

But that's not all. One assumes that Judas—who, in a way, betrayed Jesus at least less often than Peter—also wept when he saw his guilt. The difference is that Peter did not run away from his guilt, all the way into the forgetfulness of death. Peter stayed. And apologized. "Lord, you know all things. You know that I love you."

The love is more than the guilt. In fact, the love is intensified by the guilt—acknowledged, judged, atoned.

For that, Peter was sent out at the head of them, to cast fire on the earth.

Whenever I've spoken to students about responsibility over the last several years, they've groaned, "Guilt trip! Guilt trip!" Where, then, will we find men and women to cast fire into the next generation among boys and girls who cower from admission of their own fallibility, from humility before the truth, from the painfully forged spine to stand up and be counted?

Poor old Mister Guilt. I'm starting to miss him.

FIFTEEN

Teenagers and... You-Know-What

Today, if you're looking for Maria Goretti or John Berchmans, try another galaxy. In 1986, the House Select Committee on Children, Youth, and Families estimated that, in future years, we will have a minimum of one million teenage pregnancies annually, with 400,000 of them aborted and about a half million live births. In 1983, according to the National Center for Health Statistics, of the 3.7 million children born that year, 700,000 had unmarried parents: more than one-fifth. In the 1970 census, there were a half million unmarried-couple households; ten years later, there were two million. Nor do those statistics indicate how many teenagers engage in sexual intercourse without causing a pregnancy, but periodic surveys of young people are disheartening. John Gasiorowski, in *Adolescent Sexuality and Sex Education*, quotes several: intercourse before eighteen: 56 percent boys, 43 percent girls; acceptability of coitus with someone for whom you have no particular affection: 27 percent of both sexes; "I feel premarital intercourse is immoral":

(1965) 33 percent boys, 70 percent girls, (1980) 17 percent boys, 25 percent girls. Of seventy-five health clinics associated with schools across the country, 20 percent dispense birth control devices, and 50 percent issue prescriptions for them.

Why Is the Problem Escalating?

Sin. The first factor in young people's cavalier treatment of sex is the withering away of the whole concept of sin, not only in the lives of the young but in the lives of the population in general. The long lines of weekly penitents are as much a memory today as ballerina skirts and ducktail haircuts. Blessedly, we have rid ourselves of the painful scrupulosity so common among the young even a generation ago. But the price of that easement has been high: we have swung all the way from "Anything not compulsory is forbidden" to "Anything goes." In my experience, if Catholic teenagers are as sexually active as the polls insist they are, most don't trouble to mention it when they do come to confession before Christmas or Easter.

One reason, I think, is the radical change in our image of God, resulting from uncounted, subtle, mixed-blessing changes filtering down into the ordinary Catholic's understanding of God and religion—from the unread pronouncements of Vatican II, through the demytholo-gizing of Scripture, the pedestrian Englishing of the Mass, the obvious differences on moral—especially sexual—questions between ecclesiastical authorities and theological authorities, the departure of so many priests and religious from vows that were once considered irrevocable, the increase in annulments (which so many ordinary Catholics wrongly equate with "having the money to buy an under-the-table divorce"), and most especially the Church's stance on artificial birth control, which the majority of church-going Catholics seem to have rejected.

In the minds of many Catholics—especially the young—what the Church says doesn't really seem "important" anymore. To them, its doctrinal (read: sexual) stances seem too unbending and lacking in compassion to be taken seriously. What's more, they directly contradict the Jesus they encounter closer to home in homilies and hymns—the Jesus who seems to want nothing more than that we "be not afraid" and let him take care of everything. If, they argue, the official Church is "so immovably wrong about population control, it's probably wrong across the whole sexual spectrum." Thus, they simply blot out what the Church says on any sexual matter, and leave the whole thing up to the Warm Fuzzy Jesus. Consistently, young people describe God as someone who forgives anything— even when one hasn't the time or inclination to apologize. To all intents and purposes, then, there is no such thing as sin anymore.

❝ We have swung all the way from 'Anything not compulsory is forbidden' to 'Anything goes.' ❞

What's more, the young have also picked up— somewhere—the almost ineradicable conviction that all moral strictures are arbitrary and change from age to age. They seem never to have been told that sin and crime came *before* the moral strictures, that laws were written for people who can't figure out for themselves what human beings can legitimately do and not do, that it was evil for Cain to slay Abel, even though the Ten Commandments hadn't yet been published.

Young people seem also never to have heard the distinction between objective morality, which is rooted in the natures of things and human beings and which can therefore never change, and subjective morality, which is our approximative grasp of those objective natures and which surely does change from age to age. Perhaps young Inca girls did line up, yearning to be the Virgin of the Year flung from the cliff to placate the gods, but it was still objectively homicide. If objective morality is "up to the individual," then we merely had a difference of opinion with the Nazis over the debatable humanity of the Jews.

But, given that hard-headed conviction in many of the young that what the Church says is "out of it" and that morality is arbitrary and mutable, "thou shalt nots"—no matter how thunderous—simply will not work, especially in the case of sex, where there is such an enormous personal kickback.

Nor can we deal with the young on the assumption that they are convinced and committed Christians. They are baptized but not yet converted. So, if we are to convince them to live even good human lives—much less good Christian lives—we must approach them first on the level of reason, not on the level of obedience to a God they wrongly believe is a pushover or to a Church they wrongly believe is an irrelevance. Coercion motivates only when the cop is standing there. But our young are going to college, where cops are few and chastity is not in vogue. Even before that, parents surely can't be with their high school youngsters every minute of the day and night. Unless a teenager has a personally validated and internalized sexual ethic, he or she will almost inevitably "go with the flow."

Pervasive Sex. We all know that our popular culture is saturated with casual sex, but I wonder if many of the critics of religious education realize just how pervasive it is and what an enormous antagonist it is for religious educators. In my so-long-ago youth, sex was as remote and imaginary as space flight; now it is as commonplace.

Then, if you wanted to see a n-a-k-e-d body, you had to sneak a guilty peek at a sculpture book or hope the *National Geographic* soon took another intellectually stimulating jaunt to darkest Africa. Now, forty years later, any drugstore offers a cornucopia of lust varied enough to sate a satyr.

Sexual indulgence is now like air pollution or city noise or litter; we hardly notice it unless it's especially blatant. *Playboy* and its host of imitators provide not only a feast of perfectly airbrushed bodies but also enlightening articles like "What Coworkers Think (and Say) About Your Office Affair" and "The Thirty-Minute Orgasm." Everybody sleeps with everybody on the daytime soaps and "Dynasty." Ads ("Remember last night?") assume that if you enjoy someone's company, sleeping together is as natural for humans as for hamsters. The rock lyrics coming through the indispensable Walkman make the same assumption. One Rod Stewart lyric is typical: "I don't want to challenge you / Marry you, or remember you. / I just wanna make love to you." At best, that is a self-deceptive use of the word *love,* but these are youngsters who can't parse a sentence, and Tipper Gore is mocked by the young (and by the profiteers) for wanting to give parents some kind of control over what their children listen to. Proposals to put condom machines in schools are an open admission that the proponents believe the young too far gone to be convinced that abstinence is even an option.

As a result, by junior or senior year high school, having sex is as natural as cheating on quizzes. "Everybody does it." Adults are old-fashioned; what do they know about it, anyway? My mother is still a virgin.

Parents lament that so many children have no religion. But they do: paganism. If we continue under the consoling self-deception that our brainwashing has beaten "their" brainwashing, we'll continue to talk to an audience that isn't there.

Birth Control. Along with a large percentage of the adult population, the young are at least half-convinced that the pill has broken the link between sex and love. "In the old days," casual sex was taboo because the girl could end up having a baby. No other reason whatever. Now, the young believe, that consequence is easily avoidable. And parents who were themselves trained before the pill became so widely accepted are unable to give their youngsters any other reason than the one they themselves were given: the life curse of pregnancy.

❝ In my so-long-ago youth, sex was as remote and imaginary as space flight; now it is as commonplace.❞

What is odd—and tragic—is that, despite the open and wholesale talk of birth control and its easy and unquestioned availability, there were in a single year 828,124 unwanted births and 1,368,987 abortions in the U.S.—and those only the reported ones—and most of them young women. That means that at the very least two million couples believe "it can't happen here."

Freedom. The young have always wanted freedom from constraint. But that desire is exacerbated in today's narcissistic culture, in which the majority find any kind of limiting commitment repellent. "Keep your options open." Traditional parents sigh and resign themselves to turning a blind eye to the fact that "they're living together," not only without blessing of bell, book, and candle, but without any intention of more than week-to-week commitment. A survey several years ago of young men and women applying for marriage licenses asked if they thought their union would last "till death do us part"; 63 percent said, "No." And if present trends continue, at least 50 percent won't.

This delusive dream of total freedom "someday" has got to be challenged, constantly. The young forget that they will never be totally free—of gravity, of their DNA, of their pasts. Nor will they ever find a perfect liberating partner or marriage or job that eludes routine and at least occasional drudgery. They may be able to shed a spouse without too much public embarrassment, but they can never shed those years of relationship, nor will they ever be free of their relationship to their children.

Nor does freedom from outside coercion or even influence set one truly free. When a youngster goes to college, he or she will be free to skip Mass, get drunk, tomcat around—not only without the disapproval of their parents but with the evident approval and cooperation of their peers. The question is whether he or she is genuinely free to go to Mass, to stay sober, to be chaste—when the price is being labeled "nerd." Unless the youngster has a personally validated and internalized sexual ethic before leaving home, the results are nearly predictable.

Smugness. It is important, also, to remember the obvious: most teenagers are, by definition, balky as mavericks under saddle, even when there's nothing to be contentious about. More than a few come into religion class with that look which snarls, "I *dare* ya." They put their backpacks on the desk and settle in for a nice—message-bearing—snooze. They're telling you what you can do with your irrelevant and old-fashioned religion. How do you tell them they don't really understand a reality they themselves have experienced and believe they understand very, very well? Nor is your credibility enhanced by the fact that you are a celibate—which is sheer madness just for starters.

But they're not dumb. They do honestly respond when you've got them cornered, when they know they've been out-reasoned. They won't give in gracefully, but you can read the checkmate on their faces. And yet, even when you can show the selfishness of casual sex—on purely rational grounds, without any recourse to religion or authority or commandments at all—even when they get those quizzical, near-angry looks that say, "The old fool's starting to make sense again, and I don't like it," you still face the final obstacle: if they admit what you say is true (and it's beginning to look more painfully true every day), they're going to have to reassess—and perhaps even give up—something they like very, very much. And which of us humbly and wholeheartedly embraces the challenge of reassessing and surrendering something we like very, very much?

But they're good kids. Let one example stand for more than a few. A boy came to me one Monday morning and said, "Boy, did I hate you Friday night." When I asked why, he said, "My girlfriend's parents were away. And we went up to the bedroom and were getting undressed. But I remembered what you said. And I stopped. And I said to her, 'I can't. I'd only be using you.' So I got dressed, and I came downstairs, and I was just sitting there. And she came down and she said, real quiet, 'I've never been so proud of you.'"

What Do We Do?

If I am right in my judgment of the mind-set of at least a significant section of our audience, then I believe we must direct our message to the lowest common denominator: the pagans. Offer them honest, painstakingly rational motivations for sexual integrity. Not only will it not harm those youngsters who do in fact have a genuine Christian faith, but it will also give them a rational apologetic to use in verbal combat with their nonreligious fellow college students who sneer at any mention of religious motivation.

Morality/Religion. In young people's eyes, morality and religion are almost synonymous. As I've said elsewhere, their training doesn't at least seem to have convinced them that Christianity is focused on knowing a personal God and on becoming an apostle. It means to them merely being not bad. And sex is not bad; it is, in fact, very, very good. Nor do they seem ever to have heard that morality and religion are two quite separate realities, that good Muslims, good Jews, and even good atheists want to be moral—because morality is no more than what one must do to be fully human.

---

66 *In young people's eyes, morality and religion are almost synonymous.* **99**

Without any recourse to religion, a parent or teacher can show a youngster that there is something objectively unfitting about raising human babies and eating them, as if they were no different from pigs; that there is something objectively unfitting about torturing a dog, as if it had no more feelings than a cabbage; that there is something objectively unfitting about hurling food that could feed a family around a cafeteria, as if it were no more valuable than snowballs. That doesn't depend on any religion or any culture or any era; it depends on the objective, observable natures of things.

Those natures don't change from age to age. If they did, Plato would have nothing to tell us about being human, nor would our parents, nor will we. Subjective perceptions of those natures—including human nature—can change, but not the objects themselves. The rock, the tree, the cow, the human fetus tell me what they are and how I can rightly use them, not vice versa.

The same is true of human sexuality. Both animals and humans have a physical encounter in the sexual act, but human sexuality is a quantum leap different from animal sexuality. Human sexuality is also a *psychological* encounter. Animals do not perform their sexual acts behind closed doors; humans do. Why, if it's only a healthy animal act? Because, unlike animals, humans lay claims on one another, feel shame, care for one another as more than mere means to lessen sexual tension. If that psychological aspect is the specific, objective difference between animal and human sex, then to engage in sex with a partner whose name you don't even know is nonhuman, degrading both partners to the level of mere animals. That's why there is a commandment: for people who can't think.

Sexually active kids don't even realize how naively they're tipping their hands about it when they keep coming back, class after class, with, "Yeah, but if she wants it, too, then who's getting hurt?" The proper response, I think, is: "If somebody were willing to be your slave, would that make this particular slavery moral—human?" Youngsters literally gag when you suggest the possibility of bestiality. But if you don't know—or care—about your partner's hopes and dreams, what's the difference?

The young don't—or don't want to—understand that a principle applies not only in the cases you can be objective about but also in the cases where you have a vested interest.

Sex Is a Statement. Body language is precisely that: a statement. Twisting your body into knots "tells" me you're being defensive. A sneer ("I didn't *say* anything!") also tells me something; so does an upraised middle finger; and not a word was spoken. Sex also "says something." It is impossible to think of any way in which a human being can be more vulnerable than stark naked. The very situation says: "I surrender myself to you, totally." If you don't mean that, then your sexual act may be very enjoyable indeed, but it's a lie.

◇183◇

Perhaps the reason religions try to curb casual sex is not that they want to keep people from having fun. Perhaps the reason is that religions have been around a long time and have seen, time and time again, that casual sex takes something very important and makes it commonplace. What's more, they realize that sex valued solely for its own sake has no reference to the future—not merely to having and protecting babies, but to continuing the relationship itself. Two people who "make love" with "no strings" give up the right ever to be jealous.

A far more serious problem than two human beings merely acting like animals coupling arises when there is, in fact, a genuine and growing psychological commitment: "But you don't understand! We *love* one another." But to those who have had long and painful experience of it, "love" is a pretty mercurial label. It's hard to be sure that it's the right one, especially when there is such a heady personal return on a relatively minimal investment.

Love isn't a feeling; being-in-love is a feeling. Love is an act of the will. Love takes over when the feelings fail, when the beloved is no longer even likable.

If, in fact, there is a deepening psychological involvement between two sexually active partners—without any intention of permanent commitment, at least for a long, long time—then the two are drifting blindly into very hazardous waters. Not inevitably—but pretty close to it—somebody's going to get hurt.

One usually effective ploy is to blindside them. Ask them, "for no apparent reason," to describe the first time they were ever in love. Usually, it is some kind of puppy love that blazed for a while and then faded. Then you can write on the paper: "So, very often being-in-love only *feels* like the real thing, right?"

Myths. As Jesus found so often, stories are often a good end run around an audience's prejudices. Read *Tristan and Iseult* to the young—again, without any

184

previous explanation of your motive. Even the macho neanderthals see that it is a tale of terminal adolescence, that Tristan and Iseult don't really love one another: they're intoxicated by the love potion. If Tristan really loved Iseult, wouldn't he want her to live like a queen—rather than spend three shivering years in the woods eating earthworms and boiled bark? If Iseult really loved Tristan, wouldn't she want him happy with Iseult of the White Hands, once she had found happiness as the wife of King Mark? There is a profound difference between loving and simply being-*in*-love. And, oddly, the students who need the story most are the ones who understand it best—even if they'd prefer not to.

❝ Love takes over when the feelings fail, when the beloved is no longer even likable.❞

The story of Eros and Psyche is good, too. At the outset, Psyche is the unadulterated "feminine," virginal to the point of transparency. Beauty without substance, able to be worshiped but not seriously courted, a goddess without any ability for profound relationships, like Marilyn Monroe. Eros is pure "masculine," exulting in going against his mother's orders and falling in love, eager to give "the little woman" everything—except himself. It is not an adult relationship; he won't even let her see him as he really is. It is a union exclusively romantic and sexual.

Only through suffering can love emerge from being-in-love. If it doesn't, it's usually off to the divorce lawyer. Real love is very ordinary: putting out the garbage love, visiting the hospital love, cutting down on the drinking love.

Discernment. Finally, the acid test of real love is the test Jesus gave: "By their fruits you will know them." It's the same test Paul used on his feisty charismatics in Corinth: did their speaking in tongues result in more generous apostles—which would mean the gift came from God—or did it result in snobbery and disdain for those not so privileged—which would mean it was a "gift" from the enemy? The same is true of genuine, genitally expressed love: does it result in two people who are more openhearted, honest, joyful with other people outside the relationship? Or does it result in two people who are more underhanded, cranky, thin-skinned? Nifty test. And the evidence is as objectively verifiable as the numbers on a Geiger counter.

The first step toward wisdom is calling a thing by its right name.

SIXTEEN

What Does "Loving" Mean?

There is nothing our young care more about, or are more confused about, than love. Once their parents—for the youngsters' own sakes—distance themselves from the children, force them to stand on their own two feet, the young feel as lost as Hansel and Gretel in the woods or Oliver Twist alone in London. They'll fall prey to any witch who looks kindly, any Artful Dodger who will make them feel "not alone." Their left-brain education has taught them to factor quadratics and use a topic sentence, but it's never taught them what loving means. And yet we tell them that love is what it's all about.

The first step toward freedom—and wisdom and peace—is to call a thing by its right name. A skunk is not a "cute kitty"; a drunk is not "finally being himself." You can call cocaine "nose candy," but eventually you're going to find it really means a very unsweet substance that kills. Whenever you violate the truth, sooner or later the truth rises up and takes its revenge.

Probably no word in any language is so misused as *love*. It's trivialized even more than *value*. Every day you hear it bastardized: "I'd *love* a pepperoni pizza; I *love* your dress; I'd *love* to bop that guy right on the schnozz!" It's hard to think of using that exact same word to say, "I love my mother; I love my friend." Somehow, to use the same word about a pizza and about my mother is a touch obscene.

And yet we do it. Why? Because we're lazy. And many of us haven't got the words. On the one hand, there's "terrific-great-OK-not bad"; on the other hand, there's "lousy-gross-stinks-crap." No in-betweens, no qualifiers, no shadings. Also, we're not too keen on thinking, sorting, focusing the reality down to what it really is—and then finding the *exact* word that says what we really mean. That's too much like school, too much like stamping out license plates—which suggests that, for many, school was pretty much a waste of time.

Thus, we have the TV movie where two people have just finished getting rid of sexual tension together, and they call it "making love." Wrong words; no thinking. They've used the same words that two people would use who had the right to use them: two people who had shared miscarriages, kids with flu, sodden diapers, frayed tempers, bills with no funds—and yet still say, "I'm yours, and you're mine, no matter what." Something slovenly, if not downright obscene, about using the word *love* to describe selfishness.

To give the Rolling Stones their due, they never said, "I want to make love to you"; they said, "I want *it.*"

However dearly we'd like to deceive ourselves, we all know that there really is a difference. There is a very brief and animal word starting with *F* which describes a very brief and animal coupling. If that's what that act objectively *is,* why not use that ugly word? Why not speak the truth? Kid everyone else, but for God's sake, don't kid yourself.

But we have an almost infinite capacity to kid ourselves. One of the most sinister self-deceptions is:

"Where's the line? How far can I go?" Real love doesn't draw lines. Lines are for lawyers, not for lovers. "I've given my 50 percent; now where's yours?" As soon as you start asking that kind of question, you're not talking about love anymore; you're talking economics, justice and fairness, a game.

---

66 *Probably no word in any language is so misused as* love. 99

Don't get me wrong. Justice and fairness are intimately bound up in loving—whether it's the pale, thin "love" of the anonymous neighbor or the deep, vibrant love of sexual intercourse. In the sit-coms, they say, "We're going into this with both eyes open, no claims on one another, right?" Wrong. Even if I share just my lunch with you, I have a greater claim on your courtesy and concern than a casual stranger has. If you have any sense of honor, you can't claim we've never met. How much more claim on your attention and affection if I've shared my body with you, intimately, secretly? After that, you can't treat me—in justice—as if I were somebody you sort of remember from the old neighborhood. Don't call that "making love." Use the *F* word. It's closer to the truth.

Trouble is, we can share bodies without sharing selves. We can open our clothes without opening our hearts. Something dishonorable there.

The Spectrum of "Loving"

When a prism breaks white light into its rainbow of component colors, there are no hard-and-fast lines separating red from orange, or orange from yellow.

Scientists draw in those lines so that you get a clearer idea of where one color sort of ends and the next sort of begins. So, too, with loving.

You can easily separate strangers from deep friends, just as you can easily separate red from blue. But you can't draw a precise line between your affection for people you don't mind eating with and people you'd like to know better. But there is a very real difference between the words and gestures you can use with people you "kinda like" and people you'd give your life for.

The Anonymous

When we use the word *love* about "the neighbor," the anonymous people "out there," it's a rather thin reality. Still, it's love—at least to the point that we forget ourselves long enough to feel a vague empathy for the battered wife or the frog-eyed child dying of starvation in Africa. We send them money and then forget them, as we must, if our inner emotional circuits are not to burn out.

The humanity within us resonates with the fellow humanity in those suffering eyes. In our subconscious, we recall our own feelings of destitution, and that memory really does want to "do to others as you would have them do to you." It's not a guilt trip. At the very least, it's a sense of justice: a hunger to "set things right," even in a small way, for the moment. It's in our nature; it's what we were born to do.

When children are very young, parents very wisely tell them not to talk to strangers. But then they forget to tell them, when the children are old enough to defend themselves or at least to sense a threatening situation, that they needn't be so cautious anymore. When I ask students what parts of their "taped" superegos they've learned were wrong, they almost always say, "Never talk to strangers. If I never talked to strangers, I'd never have met my best friend." Not only does that wariness of strangers lead almost inevitably to a low-grade paranoia, but it also negates Jesus' command to love the anonymous neighbor. No one is in danger of joining a service project—much less the Peace Corps—who has been told, even in adolescence, to beware of strangers. The message is: take care of Number One, not the neighbor.

However, the more closely packed we become in our cities, the more suspicious we become. Truth to tell, nine-tenths of the strangers we encounter are worthy of our trust and will enrich us for opening our doors to them. But to avoid the risk of that ominous one-tenth, we keep our doors closed to all. In the old "Waltons" days, it was unthinkable to turn away a hungry stranger. Now, it would be unthinkable to invite him or her in.

The circle of loving has been dramatically constricted into a safer but far tinier and impoverishing and more claustrophobic ring. The doors have multiple locks. Curiously, the more goods we have to protect, the poorer we are in friends.

If only parents could realize that once their children reach adolescence they are more capable of discretion, then the young might be able to enrich their lives with more friends—to say nothing of being less fearful of the gospel injunction to reach out to the intimidating outcasts. When they are very young, the only thing they can understand is either/or: unless you know that Mommy and Daddy trust this person, don't get involved. Trouble is, for many (most?) people, "Don't get involved!" becomes a lifetime rule, as it was for the priest and the Levite in the parable of the Good Samaritan.

Acquaintances

There is one act without which our best friends would have remained, forever, strangers. Even before we spoke, we had to *notice* them, focus the face out of the blur of the crowd, fixate this face and body and acknowledge its uniqueness. Some are so gorgeous or repulsive or intriguing that they jump right out at you; others take effort. Then most often we exchange names. A person is now not only recognized but tagged for future reference. The relationship may never deepen, but a very significant advancement has occurred: there is one less stranger. Even if only a bit, both lives have been enriched.

---

66 *Nine-tenths of the strangers we encounter are worthy of our trust and will enrich us for opening our doors to them.* **99**

By far the majority of people we know are merely acquaintances. "Oh, hello. Good to see you again." Maybe true, maybe not, but at least it's polite; it's not self-restrictive. We may like or dislike acquaintances, but at times it is easier to be cordial and good-humored with an acquaintance than with the next-door neighbor of twenty years. Some children treat their parents as acquaintances.

Most parents fail to realize that they give their children contradictory advice: both "Don't talk to strangers" and "Don't judge anyone on first impressions"—both at once. The ads have conditioned us to quick judgments on appearances. ("No signs of dandruff, but she *is* scratching.") Yet each of us has found that, given time, some people we originally cringed from made very good friends. There are many large-hearted witches, many narcissistic knights in shining armor.

Most of our acquaintances, even the ones who have gone on to become friends, were accidental: same homeroom, same team, same office. We didn't go looking for them; we just happened to converge, because most of us are basically shy. (Perhaps the more honest word is *afraid.*) They could be bores or klutzes or leeches; they could hurt our feelings. So we rest content with a few friends. Too bad, really. In our honest moments, we know most people are "good guys." But the one or two times we have been burned swell out of proportion and dominate our good sense. And in the name of caution and safety, we impoverish ourselves.

Friends

There's a quantum leap between "Oh, yeah, I know her" and "Yes, she's a friend of mine." More has passed between these two than a mere "Oh, hi." The two have spent more time and talk together, either by choice ("I'll pick you up") or by accident ("The following have survived the cuts . . .").

The difference between "friends" and "pals" is that while you just naturally fall in with friends at a game or lunch or party, pals are the ones you just assume you're going to the party with. Friends are big-crowd stuff, not intimacy, but there is a genuine and enriching affection there. It's a good feeling to be part of something larger than yourself, and out of that larger group of friends will be distilled your "gang."

It really behooves parents to encourage (even nag) their children to join extracurricular activities at school. When I was a boy, my mother (a lady not to be gainsaid) nagged me into taking ballroom dancing lessons. I hated her for it. At first. But, against my will, I lost my shyness with girls. Far too many youngsters leave school the instant the final bell rings, thus wasting about a quarter of their tuition, but also impoverishing themselves in a less quantifiable but more profound way: denying themselves friendships and failing to develop the trust and skills to make more friendships in the future.

There are the few sad cases in every year of a boy or girl who has been so hurt by classmates in the past that he or she retreats into an anonymity that verges on invisibility. Teachers should certainly urge the more confident students to seek out the socially unskilled, just as physical education teachers should concentrate their efforts far more on the physically unskilled than on the students who already have talent and hardly need them. If Jesus' main concern was for outcasts and lepers, these are the children to whom he's specially missioned us, not only teachers but their fellow students as well.

Pals

The majority of youngsters have at least two or three pals they eat lunch with, hang out with in free periods, go to a game or movie with. Only the shyest and loneliest have the scar tissue to survive without them. There's a certain rapport and easy familiarity. And, more important, there's someone to count on when things go sour.

This intensification of friendship has moved from liking to genuine affection—sometimes even when the pal is, for the moment, not even likable. It arises from having shared more than just time and talk. Over and above the similar interests that may have brought them together in the first place, they've sacrificed with and for one another. In the fall, the football team, the play crowd, the cross-country team all hang together. Not just friends; *good* friends—who are quite likely to be in one another's wedding parties years down the line.

Here, too, there is an enlivening, enriching union, but there are also dangers: exclusivity, caution instead of risk, a smaller radius of aliveness than the youngsters could have had. "Us" not only gives the group a sense of mutual trust, but it also can devolve into being "not them." Youngsters who restrict their potential for loving only to the tried-and-true few, once again, are left impoverished as human beings.

194

What's more, we talk about our schools and our parishes as "communities" and "families." In a great many cases, not only is that metaphor a self-deception, but refusing to see that it is a self-serving lie allows us to continue rosily deceived, rather than finding the means to make the metaphor valid.

> ❝ It really behooves parents to encourage (even nag) their children to join extracurricular activities at school. ❞

What's worse, the sole purpose of our being together as Christians, whether at Mass or in school, is that we claim that the two most important obligations of our lives are to love God and love our neighbors. But you cannot love a neighbor whose name you don't even know, whose face you've never focused out of the madding crowd.

If the greeting of peace at Mass is embarrassing to many, it is because it is phony. And no one wants to admit it.

Every parish priest and every teacher should make a private vow: if I accomplish nothing else this year, I'm going to get people in my parish or school to know one another. Before Mass, encourage people to move around and meet five new people each Sunday. I have a hunch God wouldn't mind the noise, and that at the Last Judgment God will rap the knuckles of those who do mind—getting their priorities all fouled up, putting gentility above risk and privacy above loving. In class, type up a list of the students; have them check off the names of the students they've never eaten lunch with or spent ten minutes talking with; then once a week—perhaps in a lab or brainstorming for an essay—pair them up with those they don't know. They'll surely never remember the lab or the essay, but there's a better chance that they'll remember one another. And teachers will have spared themselves a divine knuckle-rapping, too.

Best Friends

Within that smallest circle are the handful of people we believe we can tell anything without jeopardizing the relationship, people we have gone not only to the circus with but through hell with—and come out friends. We've invited one another in and shown the whole soul, from basement to attic; they know all the leaks and cracks and weaknesses, and their response is, "So what?" We've arrived there when, as one student said, "You can cry together." We have found a treasure hidden in a field.

Here, too, there are dangers. Such a friend can hurt you more than any stranger can. I haven't a single such friend I haven't hurt, terribly, and vice versa. But if the love is large enough to admit forgiveness—the only love worthy of the word—then the scar tissue is an even tougher bond than before. If either side cannot yield forgiveness, then quite likely it was never love at all, but merely sloth wearing a false label.

A greater danger is the one that has threatened at all the previous levels: security by exclusivity. Everybody wants a best friend; probably everybody yearns also for a steady, a "one-and-only." Exhilarating for a while, but ultimately deadly. Anyone who grants—or demands— exclusive occupancy of that inner circle is saying, equivalently, "I don't want your life enriched in any profound way except by me." That's not love; it is, in fact, its direct opposite; call it by its right name: "distrust," not only that the other doesn't genuinely love but that you yourself are not genuinely lovable.

Many steady relationships are more slavishly monogamous than most marriages! And they are corrosive not only for the one with the collar around his or her neck, but for the one who holds the chain as well. Two people whose spirits feed only on one another's love have very little nourishment—no matter how heady—and the longer it lasts, the thinner it gets. On the contrary, anyone who sets the other free to love others, male and female, deeply and personally, gets back a friend enriched by that love.

The reason for these exclusive "pacts" is again security—which is another name for fear, distrust, and lack of faith, all of them the opposite of loving. "If I let her be real good friends with other guys, she'll fall for one of them." Maybe, maybe not. But even if she did, would you prefer *her* happiness over yours? That, after all, is what love means.

No one says it's easy. After all, this is quite often the first person in the world who ever affirmed me *as me*— and not because he or she "had to." This is the first person in the world who looked past my report card and my glasses and my acne and affirmed me—the first person who ever invited me to come in and look around, even at the less pleasant places; even my parents have never done that. The somewhat sentimental poster still tells a truth: "Set those you love free; if they come back to you, they're yours; if they don't, they never were."

Love isn't quantitative. In fact, the more you give it away, the more your ability to love increases. The basic test is giving. If that's not there, it's not love but something else masquerading under the wrong label.

Physical, Nonerotic Love

Affection is a normal, life-enriching reality. Girls are allowed to show it openly; boys are not—except for one girl, their mothers, and their dogs. Stupid, but in most cases true.

Very few boys, in my experience, can look at their best male friend and say—even in the secrecy of their own heads where no one else can hear: "I love him." All the alarms go off! "My God, am I some kind of queer?" No. A human being, doing what only human beings and no other species can do: loving. It's not only natural, it's the heart of Christianity.

---

66 Anyone who sets the other free to love others .. gets back a friend enriched by that love. 99

Touching people one loves is perfectly natural. Just because it's physical doesn't mean it's erotic. But somewhere during or just before puberty, touching becomes taboo for boys, even with their own fathers. If you touch boys, you're queer; if you touch girls, you're a rapist—like poor, gentle Lenny in *Of Mice and Men.* That natural urge for innocent body contact gets release in roughhousing and in contact sports, but in America and other Anglo-Saxon cultures, hugging a man is suspect unless you've just scored a goal—while in most other cultures, men unabashedly embrace and kiss one another in public.

Curiously, the boy who is *least* likely to become homosexual is precisely the boy who is confident enough in himself and his friends to touch them easily and nonerotically.

Physical, Erotic Love

Here, caution is not the enemy, as it has been at previous stages of friendship. Caution is the friend with the courage to tell us unpleasant truths, when we are handling not just friendship but one of the most volatile realities in human life. Oddly, however, here is where people who were painfully cautious with strangers and new friends throw caution to the winds.

There is an undeniable and healthy need to *express* love—in words, gifts, gestures, touch. If that's suppressed, it will break out elsewhere, often in unhealthy ways. On the other hand, if it's expressed too often, "I love you" becomes as commonplace and meaningless as "Have a nice day!" Similarly with sexual intercourse. If you have sex with everyone you genuinely care about, sex becomes as commonplace and trivial as shaking hands. Routine kills the magic. That's not a commandment or a parent trying to spoil your fun. That's the natures of things.

Expressions of love intensify as the relationship deepens. With strangers—"the neighbor"—one expresses love by smiling, politeness, giving them your seat. With friends there is a greater awareness of their needs, a pat on the back, jostling, fooling around. With pals expressions of love are more affectionate, leaning on one another's shoulder, a hug to praise or console. Pals know what that means; friends might not realize.

But, like the scientist drawing sharp lines on a spectrum, I have been drawing hard-and-fast categories where the realities actually fade from one into the next. Is there an element of the erotic—if only a whisper—in the rough-and-tumble games boys play? Can anyone be sure when a genital relationship really deserves the name "love" and is not really selfishness hiding behind a false label?

On the one hand, two partners in a sexual relationship can rightly say that some outsider judging the answer to that last question is precisely that: an outsider. On the other hand, the outsider might well be more experienced with the tricky aspects of personal and sexual relation-ship—and surely he or she is more objective. Moreover, in an act that has such a massive emotional kickback to oneself, doesn't the probability of self-deception increase geometrically?

Gestures and symbols communicate truth—or falsehood—just as words and definitions do. A handshake says one thing, a kiss says something more, sexual intercourse says even more: I love you, without reserve, totally. But is that what both people really mean: I love you, or I really like what we're doing?

❝The more you give [love] away, the more your ability to love increases.❞

The boys I teach hate me, I know, when I ask: After twenty minutes of heavy necking, does it really matter *who* she is, as long as she goes on doing what she's doing? Are you—honestly—doing this for her sake; is it an act of generosity? If not, don't call it love.

A good, wise friend once wrote, "It should be *difficult* to express love during sex. There's a tendency to allow the act to do the loving *for* you, and true affection (the actual love) is discarded while *you* experience the pleasure."

What's more, it's difficult to convince the young, for whom it is still so new, that there is a loving *beyond* sex. So, like my Teacher, I tell them a story. When I was born, my mother was so physically torn by the breech birth that she had to have a great many stitches. The doctor told my father that, for perhaps two or three months, he should sleep elsewhere. But, rather than take the slightest chance of hurting her or frightening her, my father stayed out of bed with her for a year.

How did he show more love for her? By getting in bed with her? Or by staying out of bed with her?

I tell girls that when guys say, "Honey, if you really loved me, you'd let me do it," they should come back with, "Honey, if you really loved me, you wouldn't ask me to prove it."

One-way streets are never genuine love.

The best definition I ever heard of real love came from a seventeen-year-old boy. He was very much in love with a girl but, as will happen, she started to get more interested in one of his friends. He told me later, not without tears, that he had said to her, "If you really think he can make you happier than I can . . . that's what I want." Is that what you mean when you say, "But we *love* one another"?

"Love is patient and kind. Love is not envious or boastful. It does not put on airs. It is not rude. It does not insist on its own rights. It does not become angry. It is not resentful. It is not happy over injustice. It is happy only with truth."

SEVENTEEN

The Journey to Justice

Justice is an instinct. At least justice-to-me is. Nobody has to teach a little girl: "Keep your mitts off my dolly," any more than anyone has to teach a puppy: "Keep your snout out of my Alpo." The territorial imperative—private property—is etched indelibly on the reptilian brain stem we share with cobras.

That one-way-street "morality" is about as far as many humanizable beings get. Some evolve further to a kind of Hobbesian shrewdness and realize that there is a certain appealing utility in détente: compromise is only a temporary loss that can turn into a later but larger profit. Fewer come to the humanizing realization that the other person is another self, not a mere appendage to one's narcissism but a person endowed with inalienable rights identical to one's own. They see we share a moral ecology in which, if one element profits unduly, another pays unduly, which is—objectively—wrong: the realization that separates humans from mere rational beasts. Still fewer take the final step to genuine Christianity and the liberating surrender: we were made by God to be servants of one another—neither lords of all we survey nor lick-spittle lackeys, but peers of the Realm, in service to the King and to all we meet. *Noblesse oblige.*

That is the evolutionary map we take on ourselves when we claim to lead the young to become good citizens and Christians.

However, there is a basic misapprehension about justice: that justice and morality have something to do with religion. Because of that misapprehension, morality cannot be explicitly taught in public schools, since it would supposedly amount to an endorsement of religion and a violation of the barriers between church and state. But justice and morality have nothing whatever to do with any religion; they are what we owe one another as fellow equally human beings. Even good atheists want to be just and moral; otherwise one couldn't call them "good." Justice and morality are what we need to keep our web of relationships—our human ecology: "society"—more or less in equilibrium. Thus, it is an anomaly that at least one purpose of general public education is to civilize the young, and yet public education is forbidden to teach precisely what civilizes human beings: justice and morality.

Moreover, even many Christians who work hands-on with the needy—among whom I include my fellow religious educators, especially those who work among the affluent needy—also believe justice has something to do with the gospel. Some, in fact, believe justice *is* the gospel. Not so at all. The Old Testament is about justice; the New Testament is about love. There is a vast difference between the justice of Solomon and the forgiveness of the prodigal father. Justice demands that once the criminal makes amends, he or she must be forgiven. Love forgives the criminal *before* he or she has merited it. Had the prodigally generous father limited himself to justice, he would not have been out every evening waiting for his boy to come home; he would have insisted on a list of crimes by species and number and would have given him a retributive and expiatory penance.

Justice and morality do not necessarily imply any connection either with religion or with love. We need merely remember the people who are, like the Pharisees Jesus so consistently castigated, as rigidly upright as marble pillars and just as unloving.

**66 *The Old Testament is about justice;*
the New Testament is about love. 99**

What's more, each of us—no matter our religion or lack of it—has a right as a *human* being to life, not out of love or charity, but out of justice. And if we have a right to life, we have a right to those things without which life is impossible: food, clothing, and shelter. Therefore, as Vatican II said forthrightly: "People in extreme necessity have the *right* to take from others' riches what they themselves need." Theft is less serious than death; life is more important than private property.

Only Christian schools take upon themselves the final stage of the map, beyond justice to loving service. But every school takes upon itself the journey to justice: to form citizens who honor our moral ecology.

Sensitizing the Soul

A primary function of schooling—public, private, or parochial—is to turn out not merely a work force at least minimally literate and skilled with numbers but a new crop of citizens who will at least respect, if not contribute to, society: our moral (interhuman) ecology. No easy task.

Perhaps nobody has to teach a little girl: "Keep your mitts off my dolly," but it takes a bit of doing to teach her to keep her mitts off other little girls' dollies. As any parent or teacher knows, civilizing a child doesn't happen overnight like puberty.

A good test of how far a youngster is along that evolutionary journey is to ask: "In a race, say at summer camp, would you give a crippled kid a head start?" It's disheartening to see even how many seniors refuse—and how loudly! It is equally disquieting to hear their facility with alibis: "Oh, he'll start expecting people 'outside' to give him the same breaks. . . . He'd feel singled out. . . . He'd be embarrassed." They *never* say, "Well, for once he'd feel he had a chance." But it's wise to know where kids are if you're trying to lead them to someplace better.

One very effective way is the Weird Monopoly Qualifier. Draw up a chart that gives bonus points for obvious advantages some people have—without having done anything to "deserve" them: height, weight, hair and skin color, family income, neighborhood, parents' education—and corresponding demerit points for those who fall short in those areas. For example, "Income: for each $1,000 over $50,000, add 5 points; for each $1,000 under $50,000, subtract 5 points." Have students add up all their scores, and the top eight qualify for Weird Monopoly. Send those eight out of class to play for the rest of the period, but they have to come back at the bell with all their properties, buildings, and money in separate envelopes. The rest of the class goes back to work. "That's not *fair!*" You're right.

Next class, the eight players "die" and pass along the results of the previous game to their "children," the next eight in the qualifier. There will be a couple of very smug inheritors whose parents passed on Boardwalk and Park Place—with hotels—and megabucks. But, inevitably, one youngster is going to end up with Mediterranean and $200. "That's not *fair!*" You're right. But Monopoly's the only game in town. Play or starve.

Monopoly starts out a perfect communism. Everybody has the same subsidy and equal opportunity. But it doesn't last even a half-hour. And in the real-life game, we all come in after it's been in progress for a long time. Thus, if you inherit Boardwalk and Park Place, you can't say to the one who inherits Mediterranean, "Make something of yourself; *I* did," because she or he can't and you didn't. Nor do any of those chosen, either day, ever realize that half the class didn't even qualify, or that in our American version the Indians once owned the whole board.

The exercise takes a bit of time, but only the ones with unregenerate reptilian brains still refuse to give the crippled kid a head start. Most are no longer as smug about welfare, realizing that children from Appalachia and migrant camps have to compete in the same game with children from Scarsdale and Beverly Hills. As Orwell said, "All animals are equal. But some animals are more equal than others."

Conscience

Invariably, when I ask seniors what conscience is, they say: "a voice in my head that tells me what's right and wrong." I wish I could find out who is going around telling them that, but even Fred Friendly, introducing the estimable "Ethics in America," defined it the same way, as if conscience were something implanted that you didn't have to wrestle for. Were that so, difficult to imagine how we got a Hitler, among many others. No, conscience is either inherited or achieved.

Most people get their consciences off the rack. When I'm talking to a boy in class about welfare, for instance, I'm almost inevitably talking to his father—and therefore often jeopardizing either his father's credibility or my own. Most consciences are an often contradictory muddle of no-no's uncritically taped on a child's superego—by parents, teachers, peers, religion, and the media. Some of the strictures reinforce one another; most jar against one another, and the person goes with the voice that is loudest, or promises the most fun, or threatens the least punishment. But one must remember that since World War II and Vatican II, we have pretty much eschewed hell as a motive, and that the principal contributor to the collective superego of our society has not been the generally civilizing voices of parents and teachers and religion but the overpowering and virtually inescapable voice of television.

> **66 Most consciences are an often contradictory muddle of no-no's uncritically taped on a child's superego. 99**

Every ten minutes, since the child was old enough to sit up in front of the electronic baby-sitter, before he or she was able to think, the child's superego was being brainwashed. No matter what the product, underneath it a voice was whispering, "The more things you have, the happier you'll be. We don't want to be like those poor children. They have no Barbie dolls and chocolate cake. The more things you have . . ." Like the children in *Brave New World* with speakers in their mattresses: "I'm a Delta-Minus. I don't want to play with those Epsilon-Pluses." Thus, without their even realizing, our young equate "good" with "rich" and "bad" with "poor"—especially if they are poor. "Oh, we don't listen to the commercials." Really? Then why do they pop into your head when you're brushing your teeth; how come you can rattle them off word for word? The best brainwashing is the brainwashing you don't know you're getting.

One would hope that a great deal of emphasis in our schools, public as well as parochial, would be to help students achieve a personally validated conscience, an explicit critique of the inherited superego tapes, testing them against reality to see which do's and don'ts are true and which are not. If not, our schools may be an at least partially successful utilitarian enterprise, training and sorting competitors and consumers for the economic system, but we have no grounds for complaint that we have too few voters and too many criminals.

As Brian Hehir pointed out so clearly on "Ethics in America," there are two quite different reasons to act morally and to treat people fairly: first, the utilitarian motives, from "We couldn't get away with it" to "But it'll catch up with us down the line"; second, the altruistic motive: "I want to be a person of character." Most dilemmas I pose to students end up hinging on the utilitarian motive. As Lawrence Kohlberg shows, the young aren't capable of comprehending motivation two developmental levels above their own, but it is heartening to see flickers of interest again and again. Or puzzlement that someone they respect might know something they're missing. Or at the very least the reluctant suspicion they just might be kidding themselves.

It seems axiomatic in our collective conscience that success is more desirable than truth, shrewdness more utilitarian than fairness, personality more profitable than character. That was one foxy deal Peter Minuit pulled on the Indians for Manhattan Island. If you trade ten nickels for your little sister's ten dimes because the nickels are bigger, that's what she wants, no? It's fair for airport concessions to jack up prices because you shoulda brought a lunch. Consistently, at least a third of students over the years have agreed that "economics should be as independent of morality as math." And it's not merely the young. I was speaking to a (more than successful) entrepreneur about the justice course I teach, and he asked what it involved. I mentioned unjust profit. Quicker than Pavlov's dog, he snorted, "There's no such thing as an unjust profit." When I proposed the pimp and the pusher, he said, "That's different." As I said, often contradictory. One-way.

Many decision makers, young and old, don't see—or want to see—that a principle is valid not only in cases about which one can be objective but also in cases where one has a vested interest. In one moral dilemma, I pose as a happily married man who loves his wife and children but is having an affair because his wife isn't very comfortable with sex and he is a very sexual man. He is, in fact, doing it "for my wife's sake, to spare her." Well, they're all over me! "Don't you realize you're betraying your marriage! And your wife's trust in you! And your whole relationship with her!" So I put on my most injured-innocent face: "But who are you to talk to me about betraying trust and relationships? Don't you ever lie to your parents? If you ever slept with a girl, didn't you betray her parents' trust in you when they let you take her out?" A whole herd of oxen gored, with one thrust! "Listen, I'm not *married* to her *parents!*" But you've had a longer relationship with your own parents than with anyone else in the world. "That's different!" Yep. It's worse.

There is always similar righteousness when the case is a fifteen-year-old girl having an affair with a thirty-year-old man. Fierce and protective indignation! Lots of exclamation points! But when I change the case to a fifteen-year-old boy with a thirty-year-old woman, every time, without a single exception, hoots and hollers of approval. Talking sexual justice to young people calls for all the same skills and patience—and determination—as arguing with San Franciscans about living on the San Andreas Fault.

The Almanac

The greatest tool I have found in breaking down the smug certitudes many of the young have picked up from

"everybody knows" is the Almanac. For a mere six bucks
a copy, I brandish a weapon to belie the belief that I'm
only saying all this stuff because I'm a priest and the
Church makes me do it and to defuse the very tricky
situation where Father is saying things directly contradictory to what the student's own father says about
capitalism and welfare cheats and justice vs. vengeance.

---

66 Without their even realizing, our young equate 'good' with 'rich' and 'bad' with 'poor.' 99

"Nations of the World," for instance, is 88 pages
detailing for each country, from Russia to Vatican City,
such facts as population per square mile, per capita
income, life expectancy, and so forth. Students are
stunned to realize life expectancy for a male in the U.S. is
72, but for a male in Afghanistan it is 36.6; that per capita
income in Canada is $13,000, while in Chad it is $88; that
if every U.S. resident got a yearly checkup, each doctor
would have to see 456 patients but each doctor in Laos
would have to see 28,000. It is equally enlightening to
discover only 17 countries have GNPs higher than the
annual sales of GM or Exxon; that U.S. air conditioners
alone use more energy than all the 1,045,537,000 people
and all the industry in Red China; and that the poorest
20 percent of Americans own the equivalent of about one-
third of the Monopoly Mediterranean card.

Welfare is the nearly uncrackable nut. O'Malley's Law:
"The less you know, the more certain you can be." When
welfare enters the picture, it invariably uncorks an
anecdotal flood, each one beginning, "Listen, I know this
guy . . ." And the guy is not only on welfare but makes
$150 a day as a caddie and drives a Mercedes with a TV

and bar in the back. Out come the Almanacs. Surprise! The only people eligible for public assistance are: children, the blind, the crippled, and the aged. Let's look on page 543. In 1987, what was the average monthly payment per family for Aid to Families with Dependent Children in New York State? The fingers move down the column. Then the heads pop up. "$490.69?" It must be a misprint. Now, divide by four weeks, then by seven days, then by four people. How much for each person per day? $4.38. And how much is one Big Mac? Also, that $4.38 has to cover everything, not just food but heat, rent, electricity, and so forth. In Mississippi, it's $1.03 a day, and in Puerto Rico, $0.91 a day. Would anybody really *want* to be on welfare?

"Most poor people are black." Nope. Check page 542. In 1986, the official poverty level was $11,203, and there were twenty-three million white people below the line and nine million blacks. The Almanac is a nifty book.

Demoralizing

It's interesting to reflect on the word *demoralizing*. When you get slapped down every time you try to stand up, staying down begins to seem the far wiser choice. When the kids in school laugh at your clothes, when your belly gurgles all through class, when you can't understand what the Anglo teacher's driving at hour after hour, dropping out seems the only sensible option. "Well, they should have the guts to make something of themselves." Psst! Remember Weird Monopoly?

I give an unsigned survey to my junior and senior classes about work, both in school and in after-school jobs. One question asks if each student is, equivalently, subsidized to the tune of about fifteen grand a year (tuition, food, clothes, and so forth): "Do you give an honest day's work for an honest day's pay?" Half say no. Well, if you who are gifted don't put in the effort to "make something" of yourself, why should someone who is definitely not gifted? How can you throw stones at welfare cheats when you're a welfare cheat yourself? "That's different!" Right. It's worse. Because you're not cheating the faceless government; you're cheating your own parents. And yourself.

I also ask my students to consider where they peg themselves among their peers as students—what their grades suggest, their parents' and teachers' expectations of them. Are you more or less content to go along with that? Think of the two or three academic hotshots in your year. Have you more or less "adjusted" to the fact that you'll never be in their number? Now try to put yourself into the pseudo-Nikes of a third-generation welfare kid. And that kid watches the same TV you do, the same every-ten-minutes incitements to permanent infantile greed. What would you say to convince him or her *not* to steal? Silence.

Demoralized doesn't mean only dispirited, limp-souled, defeated. It also means eroded morals, lax conscience, the need for vengeance. Down to the reptilian brain stem.

The Liberal Guilt Complex

If such an attempt to shatter youngsters' preconceptions and to raise their consciousness of injustices they have never even considered is effective, it can have a harrowing effect. At one extreme, the number and the variety of injustices are so enormous that many simply throw up their hands and retreat to the hypnotic solace of the Walkman. At the other, the truly sensitive stand before the throng of outstretched hands and pleading eyes and lacerate themselves with irrational guilt. Obviously, neither reaction is good, not merely for the youngster but for our moral ecology. Whichever reaction, our very attempt to raise their consciousness to injustice has lost them to our attempt to do something, however small, to stem injustice.

As Chesterton said, you've got to hate society enough to want it changed, and love it enough to pitch in and help save it. And as Eldridge Cleaver said, if you're not part of the solution, you're part of the problem.

One way is to bring in a pack of envelopes and a list of organizations, from Bread for the World to Big Brothers/Sisters. The addresses are all in the Almanac. Now pick just one and write a letter describing who you are and finish with a single sentence: "How can I help?" Now, I dare ya to send it in.

You can't crusade for everything, but if you want to share in the benefits of society—and especially if you want to call yourself a Christian—you by God have to crusade for *something,* and better for people than for whales.

PART FOUR

Passing On the Good News

EIGHTEEN

Fathering an Adolescent Boy

In all the years I've been teaching, there's been no book that can more easily make a boy say "Wow!" than *The Catcher in the Rye.* "God!" they gasp. "That's exactly how it is!" But then they're somewhat taken aback when I tell them that both Holden Caulfield and I are the same age. *Catcher* was written about *my* generation. Not much has changed in the trials and traumas and tribulations of enduring adolescence since Socrates sat around the agora in Athens, fathering adolescent boys, luring each of them to evolve an adult self.

Oh, the surfaces change. If *Catcher* were written today, Holden would probably have gone from booze to grass to cocaine to the morgue, and it would have been a short story. He certainly wouldn't have been as timid about sex. But the essential conflicts are invariant.

Here's this nice healthy little kid, comfortable with his peers and parents, as unconcerned about his looks as a bulldog, his awareness focused completely outside himself. Then, literally overnight, these subversive

distilleries in his body start shooting out magic potions—
like a werewolf at full moon. His limbs elongate and go
gangly and ungovernable; his face gets fuzzy and knobby;
and a lot of vulpine urges start whispering in hitherto
unsuspected cellars of his soul. Heaven gets blasted to
hell. He knows he's the same kid, but he's not the same
kid at all. He'd always been able to get his arms and legs
to do what he wanted them to do; his voice never played
such humiliating tricks on him; and other parts of his
body seem to have willfully independent minds of their
own, too. If the boy's parents think they've spawned an
alien changeling, how do they think the boy himself feels?

At every natural life crisis so far, a child has had to
face an unnerving change that opens up a new and more
challenging way of being human: birth itself is a traumatic
disequilibrium; then weaning and potty training; then
being shunted out to play with the other snotty little kids;
then the betrayal at the kindergarten doorway. But if each
of those crises was a mortar blast, adolescence is the
atomic bomb, because it's accompanied by the birth of
rational thought.

Before, the boy coped with those crises of separation
more or less with his intuition and gut. But this one is
almost a separation from self, and it is complicated by the
questions that have troubled the souls of philosophers
since the caves—arising in a boy whose previous questions
have been no more complicated than how to get out of
cleaning the garage and who's gonna win the Series. Who
am I? What's it all about? Where am I going? Whom can
I trust? How do I determine my worth? And for a long,
long time—perhaps even for a lifetime—the boy answers
those questions with: "I am what others think of me." He
judges himself only by externals, by the mirrors, and there
are many, many mirrors: parental expectations (real and
imagined), peers, grades, tryouts, SATs, the media. And
girls.

It's very confusing and dizzying in that hall of mirrors,
and if a boy seems as edgy and prickly as a porcupine, it's

a sure bet that, like Holden Caulfield, he's trying to find his way through the maze on his own. Every father knows that; he was there himself. Like the young Dante roaming aimlessly in the dark wood, a boy yearns for some kind and confident Virgil to come along and guide him through—and out of—hell. The lucky few find him in their father, but only if he has been playing Merlin to them from their babyhood. Perhaps more often, some boys find a guide in a teacher, probably because it's his job to continue humanizing boys when they need life lessons a woman can't give and the father is busy at "more important" matters.

❝ [A boy] judges himself only by externals, by the mirrors, and there are many, many mirrors. ❞

A boy's guide really ought to be his own father, but fathers are not only busy but shy. What's more, although little girls have been trained since their dolly-and-tea-set days to be good little mommies, nobody has trained a boy to be a good little daddy, just a good little competitor and breadwinner. And yet if Holden Caulfield's experience fifty years ago can still speak to a boy's inner needs, surely so could his father's experience, if his father could find the time to reflect on it, and put it into words the boy can relate to, and then be vulnerable enough to share his own adolescence with his son.

Both father and son tend to forget that "adolescence" is a gradual, evolutionary process, not a static stage. That suffix "-escence" signifies that adulthood is inchoate: beginning and developing, as in "convalescence." Contrary to the facts, in most cases, both the parent and the child think—or at least act as if—adulthood clicked on like a thermostat. The boy himself thinks adulthood flashed on with puberty, while his father thinks it eases on only at midnight on the twenty-first birthday or with the issuance of a college diploma. Most mothers know that too-sudden or too-delayed weaning and potty training can affect a child for a lifetime, but most fathers and sons don't realize that a too-sudden grasp of adult prerogatives (without the responsibilities) results in the dispirited, aimless high school dropout, and too-delayed grasp of adult prerogatives and responsibilities results in the spineless, whining professional tennis player.

The process is further complicated by the fact that many boys become as uncommunicative as autistic infants. If that happens, then the father has to become as subtly aware of the boy's signals as the mother was aware of the difference in the tones of his crying when he was an infant. And the kicker is that most fathers were never trained to do that either.

As boys, males were trained for competition, aggressiveness, and domination—none of which is a handy asset for fathering. As a result, in too many cases, the nurturing is left to the mother and the discipline is left to the father. It's not that mothers care more for their sons than fathers do, but more often the mother comes at the child as a concerned inquirer rather than as a worried preceptor. When the child can't articulate "where it hurts," the mother is long used to helping him in the child's own terms, while the father deals with the child most often in the father's terms. Mothers empathize; fathers tend too quickly to categorize. Mothers listen; fathers lecture. Fathers could learn a great deal about fathering from studying mothers.

I wonder if fathers and sons don't unwittingly develop a common interest in sports because it's an ideal way to be together and talk without either one revealing himself in any intimate way. No problem with that; far better than nothing at all. Just as idle chitchat is not worth recording, there is still a more significant "conversation" going on beneath it which says, "I enjoy being with you." But if that is as close as a father and son can get, the boy is left to wrestle for his manhood alone, and both father and son are missing so much of one another. Sentimental songs that ask "Where did this man suddenly come from?" are saccharine confessions that the father wasn't very much a part of his son's growing up.

The Androgynous Soul

A great deal of the unnatural dichotomy between fathering and mothering comes from a simplistic understanding of sex and gender—stereotypes that are accepted by even the most sophisticated and educated males. The female is pliable and nurturing; the male is a hard and unyielding place against which to hone one's adulthood. The female supplies warmth; the male supplies order. If you spare the rod, the kid will end up in San Quentin; if the father caresses his son after puberty, he'll wind up in some Christopher Street bar. On the contrary, a study by A. W. Adorno in 1950 found that "inmates in San Quentin prison espoused more deference to parental and other authorities" than did any other population they studied, and Dr. C. A. Tripp, who interviewed over seven hundred homosexuals and scores of field anthropologists, concluded that homosexuality has its highest incidence in macho and competitive societies such as Greece, Rome, and our own, and doesn't rise much above zero in societies that eschew heroics and glorification of the male body and its powers.

Contrary to the simplistic stereotypes, each of us— male and female—is psychologically androgynous. Every fully evolved female develops the so-called "masculine" qualities such as analysis, decisiveness, and autonomy, and every fully evolved male develops the so-called "feminine" qualities of intuition, vulnerability, and inclusive relationship. Not "Me Tarzan! You Jane!" A woman has not only a right but a natural human need to voice thoughts, beyond the cramped radius of laundry detergents and white sauce, and a man has a natural human right and need to show his feelings, beyond the cramped radius of anger and patriotism. To validate the truth of that, one need only look at the dead-ended lives of doormat women and macho men.

---

66 Fathers could learn a great deal about fathering from studying mothers. 99

No matter what our sex, each of us has a left brain which gathers, classifies, and draws logical conclusions, and a right brain which empathizes, has hunches, and makes judgments in a human context rather than strictly by some hierarchical code. A man who deals with his son only with his own "masculine" side, who approaches the boy only as a teacher and disciplinarian and not also as a fellow learner, is dealing with his son half-wittedly. And the son evolves just as half-wittedly.

How would a father react, for instance, if his son's girlfriend became pregnant? (1) Burst into fury and perhaps even into violence? (2) Sag into shame and agonize over where the father himself had gone wrong? (3) Take charge and tell the boy what to do? (4) Put his arms around the boy and weep with him, leaving explanations and recriminations and advice until the pain and shame had been shared?

Another crippling result of this one-sided teaching from the father is a conviction within the boy of a need to be perfect. It is one of the greatest—and most persistent—anomalies I've found in twenty-seven years teaching boys. No one has ever told a boy he must be perfect—surely not his parents or his teachers—and yet every boy I have ever taught is infected with the subconscious conviction that if he doesn't succeed, he won't be *truly* loved. I have absolutely no idea where it comes from, unless it arises from a fearful need in a child to cling to approval from outside, because he finds so little approval from inside.

That—combined with a lack of significant, intimate conversations with parents, in which the parents' very vulnerability to the boy is a wordless validation of his worth to them—leads to the buildup in the boy of a tyranny of wordless expectations. If fathers have forgotten how to read the smallest expressions and tics on their sons' faces, the sons have honed that talent to an art—and very often beyond, into an obsession. Every tilt of the eyebrow is a judgment, every arc of the mouth an oracle.

Perfectionism is frustrating, because it is by definition impossible for any human being. When a boy can't throw from home plate to second base, and his father says, "OK, son, then aim for center field!" that may well be a motivation. But it becomes corrosive when the boy finally is able to throw to second base—and hates himself for still not being able to hit center field.

Overly "masculinized" males—fathers and sons— seem also almost pathologically wary of touch. Some- where along the line, even fathers who have quite nonchalantly caressed their sons all through childhood suddenly stop. Both the father and the son seem word- lessly to agree that "it's not quite right" anymore. It happens sometime after grade school and the onslaught of puberty, since tenth-grade boys are constantly wrestling and roughhousing with one another—because something natural in them still craves body contact, and they have not as yet had much or any physical contact with girls.

With tragic irony, the young men who end up in Christopher Street bars are quite often men who never felt any palpable love or affection from their fathers.

By the nature of the human being, one can't deny or repress natural and harmless affection. If one does, that need does not evanesce. It retires inward and builds up steam. Sooner or later it will erupt in violence or pornography.

Even in the severely "masculine" era of the Vikings and knights, the hero knew that the sword was not enough. He also needed the gentle stirring of the harp, to give some lasting meaning to his derring-do.

Sharing Vulnerability

Even the best of fathers today have still another obstacle: the myth of the perfect father on television. Does Bill Cosby ever lose his temper? Was Pa Walton ever wrong? In the real world, you're going to make mistakes; you're not perfect either. Why try to hide the truth? If a son inevitably finds his impeccable father has clay feet, how is he ever going to put the pieces back together once the idol has toppled? Here, as before, the only sane and salvific answer is honest vulnerability.

When most fathers speak of having a man-to-man talk with their sons, they are really talking about a man-to-child talk, as if the two were still working under the same old "contract," except the boy is a bit larger. Sitting down and thinking a problem through, together—as adult with becoming-adult—will have a far greater chance of penetrating and surviving in the boy than an hour-long, self-righteous monologue. (Did it work with you when your own father did it?)

About 90 percent of teenage boys say they couldn't— or even wouldn't—talk to their fathers about anything important "because it'd just be one more hassle." A father has to remember that if a communication doesn't get through, it's the *sender's* fault. If an advertiser's pitch doesn't get across, they go back and rework the pitch. Their livelihoods depend on it. Even more true for a father: the son he loves depends on his humility and willingness to rethink.

> ❝ *A man who deals with his son only with his own 'masculine' side . . . is dealing with his son half-wittedly.* ❞

We've had the answers to fathering an adolescent boy for 2,500 years. Socrates gave them to us. The first step is to ask the student what *he* understands the question to be and—crucially —to *listen,* not with the father's understanding of the words but with the son's understanding: to get into his son's skin and listen with his ears. Only then will he know what really divides them. Unless the antagonism has gone on for far too long already, the division is rarely rooted in an Oedipal desire to best the father at any cost; it's usually a misunderstanding of the real issues—often on both sides—and a lack of experience with thinking and human living, at least on the boy's side.

Then the father can push the probing further, not with precepts but with questions: "But if you're right, wouldn't that lead to . . . ?" or "But have you thought what effect that would have on the other people involved?" The ideal father would then become more like a therapist leading a boy to a healthy selfhood than like a drill sergeant trying to nip trouble in the bud. It takes far more time than a quick "Thou shalt not," but it's time with one's son.

That ability to sit down with one's son as vulnerable fellow learner rather than as preceptor-to-receptor holds true on all issues over which fathers and sons have bickered since the caves: sex, education, religion, freedom.

Sex. The father who shouts, "Don't ever let me hear you've gotten some girl pregnant!" can be sure his wish will be fulfilled. That doesn't mean it won't happen; he just won't hear about it, or about much else important to the boy. I can't help but wonder how many abortions would never have happened if the boy (and girl) didn't have to say, "My father will kill me."

What a different atmosphere—in the home and within the boy—would arise and grow if the father had the courage to be vulnerable about his own adolescent confusions about sexuality. One of the best arguments against masturbation I've heard was in an otherwise forgettable play. The father is trying out pitches to use with his son and finally comes up with, "Son, there's not really much harm in it. But it's so goddamn . . . lonely." What if a father felt confident enough to say, "You know, I saw a woman in the supermarket today. We'd done some pretty hot and heavy necking when we were kids. She even remembered my name!"

Education. If the only question a father ever asks is "How's school?" or "How are your grades?" the son knows what's important: not learning but keeping score. As the father has long since discovered, most of the data a youngster learns in high school is utterly useless. The father himself has not found the cosine of angle AOC or use for Napoleon's dates in twenty years. The purpose of education is not to ingest data but to teach young people to think clearly and honestly. Again, what a difference if the father asked, "What are you reading in English class? Give it to me when you finish, OK? I'll read it and we can kick it around." If the father who works in the real world has stopped learning, then the boy's schooling is merely a durance vile till his father is sure the boy's thermostat has clicked on.

226

Religion. "What do you do when he refuses to go to church?" One answer I give, not entirely facetiously, is expressed in a *New Yorker* cartoon. The stuffy father is looking benignly up at his stuffy carbon copy and says, "Son, you're all grown up now. You owe me $214,000."

When the boy goes to college, he will be free to worship or not, as he chooses. But when he comes home to the tribe, he follows the tribe's customs. The boy needn't receive Communion, but he visits the Friend of his parents just as he visits the dotty old uncles and the whiskery old aunts, not because he gets anything out of it, but because he respects the people who ask him to do it. "While you're in my house, you respect my customs," just as at a Jewish funeral you wear a yarmulke.

Again, however, the father can be far more persuasive if he finds worship important enough in his own life that he has sat down and assessed why he himself believes worship something a man of honor feels compelled to do.

Freedom. The earliest years of a boy's life are shaped by his mother. When her firstborn is still hardly more than a flickering in her belly, the mother has read every book on child rearing and wearied her friends with questions. But in adolescence, when so many of the boy's confusions focus on his maleness, the mother can only yield to the boy's father. It would seem incumbent on the father to read as many books on adolescent boys as his wife read before the boy was born and belabor his friends, not with his son's SATs and stats but with questions about communicating to a rebellious alien species.

And the best-intentioned fathers have to be wary of the true nature of their task: not to bring out a new, improved edition of "the old man" but to help a boy discover what he has—and does not have—to work with in forming a unique self that has never existed before and will never be duplicated again.

One wonders how the ordinary, kindly father would react if his son came home and said, "Dad, I'd like to take ballet lessons" or "Dad, I'd like to be a social worker." It is at such moments that a man must remember that this boy is not the child of his dreams; he is the child of his love.

Legitimate Suffering

Life is difficult. Those are three words every thinking human being has had to ingest and come to peace with. But that is a fact that at least most middle-class American adolescents are shielded from by well-intentioned parents: that suffering is a natural, unavoidable part of human growth. (Can you imagine, for instance, what life would be like if all the electricity in your house went out for a week?)

❝ The purpose of education is not to ingest data but to teach young people to think clearly and honestly. ❞

But that is also a part of a father's task, to convince his son that, without legitimate suffering, one remains a petulant child his entire life. The question is not whether life is difficult or not. That is a given. The question is whether you are going to face suffering honestly and with dignity, or whether you are going to spend your life griping about it or escaping into the anesthesia of booze or drugs or casual sex. If I had to find a single cause for teenage suicides, it would be that they have been misled to expect far more of life and people than life and people are capable of delivering.

More than a few fathers have said to me, "You know, I made up my mind my kids were never going to have to wade through all the crap I had to when I was young. And

I did it. I gave them everything I never had. But . . . I didn't give them the one thing I got from wading through all that crap: spine."

Perhaps the example of the perfect father is, again, where it has always been. The good father is the man who patterns his life on the Father before whom all of us are children. Our Father doesn't fight our battles for us, but he's always there, urging us on, if we allow him to. And he never tires of listening to us. And he rarely interrupts. But if we make ourselves vulnerable to him, we hear what every son—and father—yearns to hear: "You are my son, in whom—no matter what—I am well pleased."

Perhaps the first step for a father—at no matter what cost of embarrassment to him or his son—is God's consistent way with Israel: to get him off into a place alone. Then, to put his arms around the boy and say, "Son, I know we both screw up sometimes. But I love you. God, how I do love you."

It's worth a try.

NINETEEN

P.T. Barnum and the Catechetical Quest

Just as liturgists ought to listen less to one another and more to show people, religious educators ought to cock an ear more often in the direction of salespeople—the ones who can convince loving mothers to buy breakfast cereals that will ruin their children's teeth.

Our competition—or, more forthrightly, our Enemy—has a most compelling product: "Eat (drink, drive, wear) this and you won't need God!" And, by golly, the GNP proves it works. But our Product goes directly counter to that: "Don't worry what you will eat, what you will drink, what you will wear. Seek first the Kingdom of God." That message goes hard against the grain of the wolfish id each of us harbors within, to say nothing of the competition's endless hours of brainwashing, bolstering that id's authority. But if we think we are right and the competition is wrong, we have to work harder than the competition does. And the competition works harder than Mr. Clean.

The problem isn't with the Product we offer; it's with ourselves. It's not as if we're trying to peddle Lydia

Pinkham's Pills or Fels-Naphtha Soap or Eugene V. Debs. We have a Product we claim is *the* answer to all human discontentment, a Product we ourselves have staked our lives on. And yet no one would boast that our audience is storming our churches—or our novitiates. Most youngsters today look forward to Sunday Mass as we did to Saturday castor oil. We work, obviously, in what is a buyer's market, since the overwhelming majority of our customers is buying from the competition.

Such a state of affairs would tend to give the folks at Bristol-Myers and Chrysler and Pepsico a touch of the jimjams. If most of the trade is going to Squibb and Toyota and Coke, it's shake-up time! *Nothing* is sacred but the product. So, fire the management—one way or the other; shake up the people who write the copy; ship off the whole sales force to seminars where they'll find out what we're doing wrong and come up with ways to do it right. Our salespeople are well-meaning, but they're not exactly looking back over their shoulders at the long lines of people trying to take away their jobs. And they're working pretty much in their own telephone booths, without much direction other than a new encyclopedic Catechetical Directory that would overload the mental circuits of graduate students. Our salespeople pull a textbook or a videotape off a list and cross their fingers. Of course this whole upheaval will cost, but not if both our Product and our potential customers are important. And what are we in this business for? Atonement?

Unlike ourselves, business folk don't (like the psalmist) raise their eyes to heaven and lay the blame on the unscrupulous competition—much less on the Visigoth audience. They take the minds they find, and then they make every effort to change them. Faced with almost complete indifference to their product, they don't resort to faith and hope. They call in P. T. Barnum. And if old Phineas were to carve out ten commandments to get religious education back into the competition for hearts and minds, they might sound something like the following (shorn of the cornball, and expletives deleted).

1. Presume Disinterest

Anybody in sales who doesn't presume disinterest needs no enemies. Before they arrive even in kindergarten, each of our potential buyers has logged 100,000 hours in front of the electronic teacher, extolling self-protectiveness and infantile greed every ten minutes. (They do a pretty spiffy job on the other fascinating seven deadlies, too.) If you think you can go in to that audience and be as good as "Sesame Street" with a half-hour's preparation, I have a bridge between Flatbush Avenue and Canal Street you might be interested in purchasing.

Either hook them in the first five minutes, or send them home to the competition. Consider, for instance, the pastor who climbed somewhat unsteadily into the pulpit, surveyed his flock blearily, and intoned: "To *hell* with the Catholic Church! . . . (Pause, pause, pause.) . . . So say her enemies!" Nobody's going to doze off for a while after that; there might be more.

The bear-trap opening is not merely to grab the audience's attention—although education begins with curiosity, or not at all. It also shows them that you don't take them for granted, that they're important enough for you to spend three times longer preparing the class than the class itself will take.

The best pedagogue I ever had was a Jesuit named Tom Cullen. He taught atomic physics to a class of seminarians who hoped never to hear again about Newton or neutrinos once the course had come to its unlamented close. Well, he worked: dazzling demonstrations, hands whirling like the many-armed Shiva, explanations bordering on the pornographic ("This electron's eyeing this nucleus, see? 'So, I'm . . . interested,' she says"). Rumors persisted that he rehearsed the next day's lesson alone at night in the dark classroom. We learned far more physics than we intended, simply because Tom Cullen thought both physics and we were important. And he wasn't going to be beaten.

The opposite tack is equally fruitful: think of all the teachers who insulted you and how they accomplished that. Then ask how many of those same ploys you use yourself—to save time.

---

66 *Anybody in sales who doesn't presume disinterest needs no enemies.* **99**

It might help to picture the class as, on one side, nothing but Voltaire and Madalyn Murray O'Hair, and, on the other side, Bad Bad Leroy Brown and the Laziest Gal in Town. The worse you make the picture, the better you'll be. From every group I teach, I single out the boy with the surliest look, the one who tries his best to fall asleep every day, and every night while I'm preparing, I'm pitching the course at him.

2. Be Structured, Clear, Concrete

From the first day, the class should know where the course is starting from, where it is heading, and how you intend to bridge the two. If the logical progression of the course isn't clear yet to you, expect the same of your students. And each class—no less than a banal sit-com episode—should have a rapacious beginning, a gradual build to a climax, and a knock-'em-dead conclusion. If not, the students have got better things on their mental tapes.

What is clear to an expert is not always (or even often) clear to someone whose main concerns are elsewhere. Explain the class to your spouse or to a friend. If their eyes slowly disappear up under the lids, go back and do it again, this time with nickel words. Try to adapt your language, concepts, and examples to an extraterrestrial alien. The analogy is right on the money.

3. "Ya Gotta Know the Territory"

Any teacher has to know not only the audience's resistances but also its receptivities. Don't work top-to-bottom, as we were taught; work from the bottom up. Not the evidently logical progression of the *Summa* or the catechism, but the psychological progression the audience is, at this stage, capable of assimilating. Appealing to the statements of Vatican II is as pointless as invoking the authority of the tooth fairy, when the audience is skeptical of all authority, and they hear their parents at home grumping about the pope and the pill. Listen instead to the music young people listen to more than they listen to us. Read Judy Blume, not because she has the answers, but because the kids we teach think she has the answers. At the very least, she knows where the pain and uncertainty are.

Most of our students, in my experience, are polite, well-groomed pagans with Christian labels. They are motivated, for instance, in their choice of careers by values no different from those of the pseudoatheist student in the public school down the street. The choice between a $15,000 job teaching English or a $30,000 job writing ad copy for floor wax is scarcely a choice. Many of them believe that being spoiled is an incurable disease, and if they haven't yet been afflicted with it, they want to catch it as soon as possible. Within ten years of graduating college, they will be living better than their parents do now.

Oddly, that plays right into our hands. The competition has overdone it. Why? Because it simply doesn't work. In the first place, if material comfort fulfills all human hungers, most of us already have material comforts (barring, of course, the immoral) greater than any caliph of Baghdad ever enjoyed. Why aren't we all biting our toes with bliss? In the second place, Elvis Presley and Marilyn Monroe had money, fame, sex, and power that still lasts, decades after their deaths. Difficult to figure, though, why people who "had everything" would kill themselves.

What's more, it is not difficult to show students that the result of the competition's brainwashing is a pervasive self-distaste that imbues most of their waking moments. Everybody else's face, body, clothes, parents, and prospects are inaccessibly "better" than theirs. Runaway competitive capitalism has turned them into donkeys with carrots dangling in front of them. And they run, and run. And run. Our task (even against our own training—and especially against their parents' training) is to convince them that it's enough merely to strive. They don't have to achieve.

In the competition's cosmology, "failure" took the place of "hell" and "sin." But if, in the Olympics, even the silver medalist is a kind of failure, then just about everybody is to some degree in hell and sin. It is the liberating message of the gospel that—like Peter, the klutz, and Jesus, the crucified—we "win" merely by refusing to give up.

One very touchy point is worth working on: the difference between guilt and responsibility. Like doubt, guilt is a very salutary feeling—provided the cause justifies it and provided it turns into responsibility. But the guilt is worthless—in fact, corrosive—until one takes responsibility and does something about it.

4. Teach Students to Think

It's not enough to know that TV has pandered to the natural law of inertia and made students even more passive. On the one hand, it is not helpful to give them a steady diet of films, going in their door and staying there: "OK, kids. Today we're going to see a videotape and pool ignorance about it."

Nor, on the other hand, is it helpful to go to the opposite extreme and drill into them the dates of Nicea, the ways in which the Persons of the Trinity coexist, and the grounds for legitimate annulment. I think back on the three years of philosophy and four years of theology I endured, and I'm hard-pressed to come up with more than a handful of data that I ever found useful. Can you? It's all "changed," hasn't it?

---

66 Any teacher has to know not only the audience's resistances but also its receptivities. 99

There is, of course, a core body of data about Christianity and Catholicism that is essential if any young man or woman is going to make an informed choice of Christianity and Catholicism. It is in the Apostles' Creed— and even much of that can be left to college or even graduate school. Those years of intense theological study didn't implant *The Catholic Compendium* in my brain. They taught me (1) how to think clearly and honestly and (2) where to look for the data.

We must convince students to think and argue not only clearly but also honestly—and to realize that the truth, no matter how disconcerting, can never threaten religious belief, no matter how painfully it forces us to rethink and reformulate. And, most important, the object of our search together is to find that truth, not to win.

Beyond that, we have to show students where to find the data when the problems become real: *The Catholic*

Encyclopedia (for starters), *The Dutch Catechism,*
McBrien's *Catholicism, The Jerome Biblical Commentary.*
While we still have some entree to their minds, we have
to give them problems—meaningful to them, where they
are now—and challenge them to find answers we can
critique with them, rather than outfitting them with
ready-made, unsatisfying, and ultimately dismissible ones.

We cannot share our faith with them. We can share
only our knowledge of the options.

5. Be Flinty and Vulnerable

In the search for an authentic self, young people need
a hard place against which to hone their adulthood. We
will not achieve their trust by presenting them with a
roll-over Jesus whose only message was turning the other
cheek. The result of a decade of that message is the
vacationing Catholic who believes God will forgive
anything, even when one doesn't have the time or
inclination to apologize for it. The gospel is a challenge to
everything our students consider unchallengeable—as did
the first disciples: "Who will have the first place in this
new Kingdom?" Much to our chagrin, Jesus answers that
with: "Whoever takes the last place; whoever serves all
the others, especially those unworthy of it." If that gospel
doesn't unnerve our audience, then they haven't really
heard it. For which we can blame a sales force too fearful
of scaring them off, too untrusting to see that our
audience is, beneath the surface "cool" and condescension,
brother and sister to Odysseus and Antigone: "So nigh is
grandeur to our dust, So near is God to man, When Duty
whispers low, 'Thou must,' The youth replies, 'I can.'"
Joan of Lorraine was an unlettered peasant girl, but look
what she did to someone as wimpy as her Dauphin.

But our students must also sense that we, too, have
been afraid, screwed up, in league at times with the
competition. They are already too afflicted with the
frustrating perfectionism programmed into them by

competitive sports, the SATs, parents' unrealizable expectations of them. "I had problems with masturbation, too; I lost my head over boys, too; I felt like cheating, too. But I'm still here." In our study of Scripture, it is not unprofitable to reflect on the fact that God has always had a penchant for the nerds, wimps, and nobodies: Noah and his eccentric brood, barren Sarah, stammering Moses, spindly David, lepers, grafters, whores. We are challenged by a God who makes miracles even with mud and spittle—provided we forget our shortcomings and allow ourselves to be used. Beneath the nubs and knobs of every toad, our Father sees a prince or a princess.

6. Show That Suffering Is Inescapable

Life is difficult. Suffering is a natural factor in human life and human growth. It arises from the imperfect way in which we are made (*so that* we can grow) and from interaction with other different, self-willed, imperfect persons. But, as M. Scott Peck says, avoiding the risk of suffering is so pervasive it is practically a characteristic of human nature. And yet calling it "natural" doesn't mean it is salutary or unchangeable. "It is also natural," he says, "to defecate in our pants and never brush our teeth. Yet we teach ourselves to do the unnatural until the unnatural becomes itself second nature." Unlike animals, we are not compelled to adapt to our nature. On the contrary, our humanity itself is an invitation to transcend our nature.

And Christianity invites us further, into the super-human aliveness of God. But as the story of Adam and Eve and the contrasting story of Jesus prove, unarguably, there is no going round humanity to divinity. And humanity—and its growth—are inextricably bound up with suffering. If Christianity offers nothing else more compelling than any other world religion, it offers a God who was tempted to despair: "My God, my God! Why have you abandoned me?" *But:* "Into your hands I commit my spirit." Our God does not demand superhuman courage. Coward's courage is enough.

7. Offer Concrete Ways to Serve

I bristle at well-meaning educators bent on "conscienticization"—and for more than that jaw-breaking buzzword. With a surfeit of zeal and a dearth of common sense, they set children ablaze with a righteous awareness of the global inhumanity that people inflict on others—and then give them no concrete outlet by which to purge their newfound sense of responsibility. A cannister at the cafeteria checkout, soliciting funds for the starving, is a worthwhile effort, but these are youngsters geared by every agency around them to judge value by concrete results. Wrongly, perhaps, but they are just lurching toward conversion, remember. In order to be sustained in their rudimentary experience with self-forgetfulness, they need more than hearing they can make a difference or they have made a difference. They must *feel* they have made a difference, if—once again—we are going to render ourselves unnecessary.

> **❝ Our humanity itself is an invitation to transcend our nature. ❞**

Even for the students too young to leave the school for a service project, there are more than enough outcasts, right at their elbows: the girl who eats her lunch every day alone, the boys you know on sight were the first ones hit in the grade school dodgeball games, the boys who have never been asked once to a movie, the girls who haunt the corners of the dance—huddling together and giggling and pretending they're not yearning to be asked to dance, just once. Pick a youngster you sense may be on the verge of Christianity: "Psst! See that kid over there who's all knees and elbows, hoping he won't get picked for the softball game? Take him over there and show him how to throw a ball the right way, OK? Maybe fifteen minutes? Dare ya."

8. Don't Turn Out Half-wits

Each of us has two brain lobes. The left brain gathers the data, and so on; the right brain puts the pieces back together, incorporates the new learning with what's been learned before, sees the significance of it to one's life.

Even though students can't remember the left-brain stuff, even from year to year, most schools do a creditable job trying at least to "cover the matter assigned." We have textbooks to "get through"; we have tests and grades to prove to the office we are not airheads. If we don't, we'd better get cracking at that.

But if all our religious education students take from us is the miniscule bundleful they've been able to remember of the left-brain component of our courses, we might as well all go looking for jobs in pornography mills. Unless we have shown Christianity as meaningful in their lives, we've done little more than baby-sit.

Jesus wasn't a speculative theology teacher. He was going for the heart. Therefore, a good part of our efforts must go into finding ways for our students to *experience* both God and community. All the "proofs" of Saint Thomas, all the arguments, all the debates are good seeds, planted but unwatered. Without discovering God through prayer and retreats, all our classes—no matter how engrossing, structured, clear—are as academic as history and about as likely to affect the personal lives of those we teach. As few will become committed Christians as will become professional history professors.

Our task is not simply to challenge the mind. Our task is also to move the heart.

9. Conduct Periodic Audience Polls

If your faculty is fearless enough to allow them, give periodic polls—and not just the year-end evaluation. If you give periodic quizzes on the content of the course, give your students a few minutes at the end to reply to: "How is the course going? Too fast, too slow? What did you like most? Least?" Vulnerability is, after all, what we preach, and it is a ploy our audience is quite unused to.

Another method—very time-consuming for the teacher, but very valuable for the students we are here to serve—is a journal which elicits student responses to the questions the course is dealing with. It has several advantages. First, it subverts the lesson most students learned at least by fourth grade: never raise your hand; never make a comment; if the teacher calls on you, look at the floor long enough and he or she will ask somebody else. Second, it forces students to focus what they do really know and believe; if they can't put it into words, they don't really know it. And third, it allows them to throw their ideas up against a mind that cares for them and for their ideas. As long as they are civil, they can say—or raise—anything they want. And if they are uncivil, that tells the wise teacher a great deal, too.

10. Show Students Your Love

Father Flanagan of Boys Town was right. There's no such thing as a bad boy—or girl. Hurt, maybe. Confused, angry, perhaps even sick. But never bad.

Perhaps P. T. Barnum is not the right spirit to invoke in our need. He was governed too much by sheer *numbers,* by the ticket stubs from the "suckers." We don't want suckers.

But, then again, perhaps we do.

TWENTY

The Adult Christian

With a penchant for paradox well-known to readers of the Hebrew Scriptures and petitioners at Delphi, God gave us the freedom to manipulate objects in any manner we can imagine—and then gave us objects that can be manipulated in only one way without setting off a built-in "tick-tick-tick." Skinny-dip with piranhas; bury nuclear waste; pinch Krazy-Glue; trust the Ayatollah; put nightshade on your Wheaties. Just don't expect to get away with it. Violate the natures of things, and sooner or later the natures of things rise up and take their revenge.

No need for hell. No need even for a cop. Like the headache in the fourth martini, the punishment is tick-tick-ticking right there inside the crime.

Thus, I would submit that if the official Church continues to take for granted the simplicity of its audience—tick-tick-tick. You can't treat adolescents like children or adults like adolescents. If you do, they will either leap the fence in rebellion against the boredom and irrelevance, or they will stay behind because they are content with boredom and irrelevance, and we will have a church of contentedly unprofitable servants.

Erik Erikson makes a convincing case that an unhealthy soul is the result of growth refused—or forbidden. He shows that, by their very nature, human individuals and human enterprises inexorably encounter disquieting challenges, moments of disequilibrium that taunt us to reshuffle all the old formulas and certitudes, to leave behind the comfy cocoon and learn how to fly. Each moment of disequilibrium is a catalyst that can lead to new growth or—rejected—to stagnation and even to despair. Doubt can be life-giving; inflexible certitude is certain death.

The divinely ignited pubertal disequilibrium for the American Church, the death of its former malleable innocence, was quite obviously the hurricane of Vatican II. What's more, Vatican II coincided, within a single generation, with a host of other disequilibriums—none without Pentecostal possibilities: race, feminism, the pill, the omnivorous media, the Third World, divorce, drugs, Vietnam, living together, Watergate, assassination, the naiveté of Woodstock and the murderous cynicism of Altamont, the geometrically burgeoning bureaucracy that daily persuades us that the individual never again will be able to make a difference. Everything seemed up for grabs; we had to go back and refight all the old battles we'd thought were settled—just as every adolescent does. But the alternative was to remain childish till death, to subvert the natural law of self-transcendence built into our very human nature.

I realize now that, twenty-five years ago when I returned to the seminary to study theology during Vatican II, the pronouncements of the Church *were* my conscience, a superego taped as uncritically as any child's entering elementary school. I was thirty years old, and yet my understanding and my certitudes were no more adult than any child's memorizing the catechism: the sanctity of Saint Christopher and the divinity of Christ were equally unquestionable; eating meat on Friday and fornication were equally punishable. Every verse of Scripture was literally true, and even though I had studied both evolution and nuclear physics, I knew that at one time snakes used to talk to naked ladies in the park and that Jesus rose straight up to heaven without going through the Van Allen belt. The left side of my brain was incommunicado from the right side. And both were content—or at least walled off from one another, like a knight and his lady on either side of a bundling board.

❝ Like the headache in the fourth martini, the punishment is tick-tick-ticking right there inside the crime. ❞

Then, suddenly, they weren't. Someone yanked the board. "Something there is that doesn't love a wall." Hindsight tells me that that something was the will of God, written into the natures of things and human beings—even of the mystical body of Christ.

And if that traumatic disequilibrium staggered a seminarian who had John Courtney Murray and Avery Dulles and Joseph Fitzmyer to help him grow up, what of those laypeople who had not had the daunting privilege of reading Raymond Brown, Karl Rahner, Henri de Lubac, and the other scholars who led me? And what of priests who had nothing more than the theological manuals, with their "notes" telling the degree of utter certainty of each thesis?

How many American practicing Catholics have wrestled with—or even heard of—the synoptic problem or probabilism? How many are there whose last—and definitive—encounter with theological questions antedated the disruptions of the 1960s? How many face these new issues with no more than a catechism they fear is now "discredited"? How many are there whose act of faith rests not on the data, personally examined, but on the teaching of the Church—which now seems to be very confused, or at least confusing, indeed?

As in adolescence, not only all the old certitudes were trashed, but also, perhaps even more important, all the old landmarks and symbols of the simpler Old World faith: benedictions, rosaries, novenas. Even the Mass suddenly and for no apparent reason became "the liturgy." Powerful personages, somewhere, rearranged the whole thing to be historically "correct" and psychologically barren, as anesthetized as a play written to embody the atomic theory. De-Latinized, the Mass became both more accessible and more banal, sacred mysteries in name only, and the word most often used about them—by the old, mature, and young alike—is *boring.*

Being a lifelong student of ways to ease adolescents through the trauma of their disequilibrium, I found myself wondering whether anyone in the Church was worrying about those people—that is, the majority of American Catholics. In our much-publicized attempts to influence what a good adult Catholic does in the bedroom and boardroom, what a good Catholic thinks about peace and economics and the Third World, had anyone given any thought to helping them with a far more fundamental problem: how to be a good adult Catholic?

Then I was struck by the frightening possibility that the parental Church was treating adult Catholics—even those with advanced degrees—in precisely the way those same Catholics were treating their own adolescent children: not as adult-to-adult but as adult-to-child.

Many people who feel a deep loyalty to the Church as their mother are labeled fifth columnists when they aver that God gave humankind intelligence and invited us to use it, long before God found need to give us a magisterium or even the Ten Commandments. Many who found themselves intellectually at odds with the mother Church—including many priests and religious—"left" the Church; the rest said, "To whom shall we go? You have the words of eternal life," and they stayed. But one would be foolish or blind to say that those who stayed form a lively sheepfold.

Although I doubt anyone can "leave" the Church, any more than one can "leave" his or her family, many don't return even for the holidays. I suspect most nonpracticing Catholics did not storm out of the house in anger. They merely stopped coming around, not because the Church was wrong, but because, in their eyes, the Church was irrelevant to life as they perceived it.

Those who drifted away have not done so because they found something better. They've merely shucked off the moral corset of "all those rules" (which ones, they rarely seem able to specify other than birth control), so that they seem more like discontented runaways than liberated thinkers. One even wonders whether in any real sense they were able to leave the Church, since they seem never truly to have been "in" it.

The departed seem merely to have settled for the prevailing ethos—not "liberated" but just "not bound." Without a coherent, personally evolved ethic or world-view, they are fragmented, reactive, adaptable, open-minded—in an old-time formulation: prime matter waiting for someone outside themselves to impose a form on them.

In escaping the unexamined superego they believe the parent Church "brainwashed" into them, they have traded a sharply focused guilt for formless anxieties. They have transferred their dependency from paternalistic and flinty priests onto companionable and nondirective therapists, who cannot provide an organic meaning to their lives but only methods to cope with their symptoms. The natural human hunger for self-transcendence is palliated with the same placebos everyone else is taking, and narcissism fills the spiritless void.

Nor are those who remained within the visible Church much better off. We still share that same world, in which everything is scrupulously demythologized and thereby trivialized: heroes, women, miracles, sex, old age, work. We have been socialized by the same agencies to believe that nice guys finish last, that cool is in and vulnerability, awe, and faith without guarantees are less likely to come back than Halley's Comet. The fact that we stayed is, in my mind, some kind of moral miracle, because it is a pretty tall order to sell faith to people so schooled by our shared history to skepticism, cynicism, and low-grade paranoia.

> **66** *Those who drifted away [from the Church] have not done so because they found something better.* **99**

There we find the real enemies of the postadolescent American Church, and its greatest challenge: not the condom makers, but cynicism and impotence, a sense of personal meaninglessness. In the whirlwind world of megagovernment, megacorporations, megadeaths, how can any individual say he or she makes any significant difference? In the rush to demythologize, is there anything still "sacred"? Anyway, in the midst of the smothering anesthetics (including too often even our worship), is it even possible to clear a place from which one might sense a communion with "the living freshness deep-down things," with the *Logos* who gives meaning even to what seems to us senseless, whose first and continuing act is to bring cosmos out of chaos, and in whose image we are made?

That is what those who remained come to church to find, no matter how unarticulated that need might be: a sense of personal wholeness and, beyond that, a sense of an outwardly radiating self that extends to the worshiping community and further to the human family and beyond time into the life of God.

I fear precious few find it. There are good parishes; there are exemplary parishes. But they are all too few. What those who seek meaning in the postadolescent American Church find too often is a liturgy that is childish and a homily that itself is a parental placebo, without challenge and very often embodying the very competitiveness and materialism the gospel decries. Even the classes of university professors are sometimes visited by the dean; judges and politicians are monitored by the press, doctors and businesspeople watchdogged by the law. Clerics are not.

When my students ask what would reenliven the American Church, I answer, an atomic war or a worldwide economic depression, neither of which seems totally out of the question. One priest, whose opinions I honestly respect, said, "You're asking laypeople to be theologians, which they can't be. That's the service the Church provides them." And therein, I think, I found the kernel of a more serious answer.

If the American Church is to become adult, as its members are adult, then—radical or even Protestant as it may seem—I think we must turn the American Catholic into a theologian.

I do not mean to usurp the authority of the Vatican. I do not mean even to usurp the authority of the professional theologians. In this day of specialization, no one can hope to be an expert even in the most important fields of human life. But that is no reason the man and woman in the pew must leave custody of their minds and hearts and souls in the hands only of the magisterium or the professional theologians—as they must leave their carburetors and cardiograms in the hands of unquestionable authorities. They have a right, as intelligent and free adults, to a second or third opinion.

The first obstacle is to persuade people that doctrinal, moral, and scriptural questions merit at least as much time in their week as "Monday Night Football." An adjunct problem—not only for the laity but also for clergy—is the conviction that theology is the service the priest offers the people of God. Most priests are not primarily theologians, either. Their ministerial work focuses more on counseling and consoling than on explaining doctrine or testing its limits.

Especially with the dwindling number of priests, adult Catholics must realize they have to take on themselves more responsibility for their own evolution as believers.

The next task is to provide meaningful—and appealing—forums in which intelligent, adult Catholics can probe their faith. If growth in understanding is an indisputable requirement of the natural law, and if understanding our Christian faith is important, then the choice is clear.

Adult education is essential not only for the adults but also for their children. If the lack of priestly and religious vocations tells us anything, it tells us that, even to the most intelligent and best motivated of our young, a career in the Church is uninviting. If, despite the best efforts of dedicated elementary and secondary school religious educators, our young still believe being Christian means little more than being well-mannered, then the enemy's propaganda is far better than ours. And our schools are dwindling; more of our young go to secular schools; CCD does more to placate the guilt feelings of parents and pastors than to answer the needs of the young. Then the parents must learn, in order to teach.

Except for one I gave myself, I have never heard a homily wherein the priest suggested a book—or provided a list of theologically oriented books (including novels) at the exit of the church. Perhaps there are book reviews in some diocesan newspapers, but I can't recall ever having read one. The closest I've come is a good priest who tries to have people subscribe to tapes of Bishop Sheen's talks from the prepubertal fifties.

---

66 If the American Church is to become adult . . . I think we must turn the American Catholic into a theologian. 99

I am not asking for reviews of the latest Hans Kung or Charles Curran, though that is not out of the question. But how many postadolescent American Catholics might be lured toward the more complex theologians by *The Road Less Traveled* or *Habits of the Heart?* Or by Graham Greene, John Updike, Flannery O'Connor? Stories were Jesus' own method of preference for conveying the gospel. And, say what you like about Andrew Greeley, he gets the readers—and many of them postadolescent Catholic readers. Come to think of it, I can't remember the last time I heard anyone suggest from the pulpit that a subscription to *America* or *NCR* or *Commonweal* might raise the adult level of a Catholic's thinking.

Without that, despite our progress, despite our prosperity, our churchgoing will be only self-delusively different from the meetings of Samuel Beckett's lonely clowns, not a celebration of unity, or victory over death and meaninglessness, or our sense of mission to bring cosmos out of chaos, but an act of bleak hope.

Till then, tick . . . tick . . . tick.

TWENTY-ONE

Making Parents Apostles

In all the talks I've given from Minneapolis to Melbourne, parents inevitably ask, "How can I get my teenage children to Mass?" That consistent question suggests several things: first, that Mass is a "celebration" young people from here to the antipodes don't relish; second, that parents believe just getting kids to Mass is about the limit of their obligation as the primary religious educators of their children; and third, that parents leave everything religious beyond external compliance to the schools or CCD.

One mother in Sydney put the problem clearly and forthrightly: "I simply don't feel competent to deal with my kids' religious questions." The harsh answer that popped out of my mouth at that moment is still the only answer I have: "If your kids' souls are at least as important as watching television and learning how to fill out tax forms, then *get* competent."

Parents are—or ought to be—the principal educators of their own children, and they can't legitimately leave their children's minds to teachers the way they leave their carburetors to mechanics. If parents disapprove of *The Catcher in the Rye,* for instance, I'll continue to teach it, but I have no right to demand a student read it if his or her parents object. On the other hand, don't blame me that your son or daughter doesn't want to go to Mass or finds Madonna a more appealing role model than Our Lady; you've had them for seventeen years before they come to me, and you have them eighteen hours a day, while I have them for only four hours a week. What's more, what a parent says—and does—most often carries more weight than what a teacher says and does.

---

66 *Parents . . . can't legitimately leave their children's minds to teachers the way they leave their carburetors to mechanics.* 99

However, by far the majority of the students I've taught believe their parents don't want to talk about "religious stuff," or say that raising such issues triggers silence, accusations, or homilies starting with "When I was your age . . . ," or that parents subscribe dully to some "old-time religion" in which questioning or doubt is equivalent to disbelief, or that their parents simply wouldn't know the answers to religious questions. In a review of research on the family's influence on adolescent sexual behavior, for instance, S. Shelly reported that fewer than half of teenagers polled actually communicated with their parents about sexual matters and 25 percent never communicated at all. Moreover, I often find that the competitive, materialist worldview coming from the media (which is my most powerful opponent in religious education classes) is precisely the worldview many parents espouse: "Social worker? How much money can you make doing that? . . . Holy Cross? Are you crazy? You've been accepted at Bucknell! . . . A year in the Peace Corps will stall your career!"

But the answer I'd given the lady in Sydney—"Get competent"—boomeranged back at me in another equally forthright question: "How?" she asked. Which left me with this essay to write, for parents who genuinely believe internalization of religious values is important for their children (and for themselves), and for parishes that want to help parents become our fellow apostles—and an inestimable help to religion teachers.

Getting Competent

Most parents left learning more about the God and Church questions back in college theology courses or dorm bull sessions. A definite minority do subscribe to *America* or *Commonweal* or *NCR,* and fewer still buy and read books dealing with religious questions—though I've never heard a homily exhorting them to do that. If they read anything at all dealing with the Church, it is diocesan newspapers which, in the cities where I've served, are usually theologically both hypercautious and hyper-surface. In one way, that is understandable. The Church most of us grew up in acted as if religious knowledge were like the Deposit of Faith: all questions "covered and closed" by the end of one's formal education. The idea that anything new might be unearthed regarding the God questions or that new avenues to deeper religious insight might develop never crosses the minds of the majority of Catholic adults. What's more, the "real world" outside the halls of ivy is a jungle where more concrete and pressing questions and decisions co-opt most of our time, a world of cutthroat competition, specialization, and information glut, with simply no time to keep up even with one's own field—much less the latest on infallibility, in vitro fertilization, and the use of symbol and myth in Scripture. That's what priests are for.

But there's one major factor left out of that alibi: our young. A parent can be rightly proud of his or her job teaching children mannerliness, diligence, fairness, and the other virtues even good atheist parents try to cultivate. But unless they also help to pass on the faith, unless they take time to learn—or relearn—theology in order to teach it, they have no right to complain that "they've left the Church, after all that tuition money." As Eldridge Cleaver said, "If you're not part of the solution, you're part of the problem."

In chapter one of this book, "Selling Faith to Skeptics," I offered five basic questions religious education ought to address in order to help parents narrow the baffling scope of religious education to a manageable size. They could serve as an outline here: (1) What is human fulfillment? (2) Is there a God, and, if so, what is God like? (3) How can I relate to God personally? (4) Why an organized Church? (5) How does belief in God change my relationships?

Most busy parents are not ready for the documents of Vatican II or the latest Hans Kung. Two books I have found helpful for myself and for my students and their parents are McBrien, *Catholicism* (the one-volume paperback edition, Harper & Row, 1981) and *The Dutch Catechism* (Seabury, 1969). Although they are not definitive nor perhaps even the best available, they do provide a thorough overview or quick reference.

Human Fulfillment

The first question is a pretheological one; in effect, why even bother about theology if you can live a happy and quite successful life without it? What, in fact, does the word *success* really mean? If most of us "unpacked" that word, I suspect the contents would have more to do with Amana refrigerators and suburban houses and "The Tonight Show" than with integrity and a consistent worldview and a relationship with our Creator. It would be the question pastors would have to face in order to convince parents that they themselves need updating in theology from hardly remembered and probably quite dated, oversimplified texts and insights.

> **❝ Most parents left learning more about the God and Church questions back in college theology courses. ❞**

In a very real way, many of us have simply succumbed to the prevailing materialist, hedonist, narcissist ethos and values of our time and, without our realizing, it is an ethos diametrically opposite to Christianity. We have insulated religion from "the real world," so that the only time we consider the God questions is (perhaps) an hour on Sunday, and the rest of the week we govern our choices and behavior by the same norms as the well-intentioned pagans or atheists down the block. Our youngsters' choices of colleges and careers, for instance, are likely based on motives as hard-nosed and pragmatic as Gradgrind's in *Hard Times* would have been. We deal with facts, and facts have more to do with the Gross National Product than the Sermon on the Mount.

But if money-fame-sex-power are the key to human fulfillment, consider Elvis Presley, Marilyn Monroe, James Dean, Jim Belushi, Jimi Hendrix, Janis Joplin, Jim Morrison, and a host of others, who had money-fame-sex-power full measure and overflowing, yet still killed themselves. So much for the validity of the materialist life view. But I would further suggest *The Road Less*

Traveled (Touchstone, 1978), by M. Scott Peck, a
psychiatrist whose book has been on the *Times* best-seller
list since God was a child. Quite accessibly, he tells about
what "growing up" means and how religion helps that not
inevitable process. Also, Robert Bellah et al., *Habits of the
Heart* (Perennial, 1985), points out how Americans have
given up the pursuit of goodness for the pursuit of feeling
good. But if there were only one book a parish discussion
group or individual parents needed to convince them of
the hollowness of the American dream, I would recommend Lasch, *The Culture of Narcissism* (Warner, 1979),
which relentlessly savages the self-deceptions of our
economic, educational, athletic, sexual, and psychological
"values." Lasch does not say what should take their
place, but he sure as shootin' shows they don't do what
they purport to do. Show parents Paddy Chayevsky's
masterful satire on our media values: *Network*. It is
a fine video to view back-to-back with *A Man for All
Seasons* or *The Mission*. Somehow, the human spirit—
no matter the yowling distractions—is still down below,
mewing helplessly in each of us, "There's *gotta* be more
than this!"

According to Jesus, there is only one touchstone of
human success: "I was hungry, I was thirsty—what did
you do about that?" In my experience, that is not the
touchstone most students—or their parents—use as the
norm of human fulfillment.

The Existence and Nature of God

Most of us operate from the unexamined premise that
there simply must be a God. A great part of our conviction
is merely trust in our parents and in kindly priests and
religious, but few of us have faced the possibility that that
trust might be misplaced. After all, "everybody said" the
world was flat, and they were wrong. If God actually does
not exist, all our belief will not make God exist, any more
than our ability to draw unicorns will make them trot

silver-hooved out of the woods. If God does not exist, then all the scriptures of all the religions that ever existed are just so much self-delusive wastepaper. When Charlie Brown asked Snoopy the title of his theology book, Snoopy wisely typed, "Has It Ever Occurred to You That You Might Be Wrong?" Unless you've entertained the possibility that God does *not* exist, you don't choose to believe in God freely; if two roads diverge in a yellow wood and you know of only one, the road you take is not taken freely.

To face the question squarely, I suggest Beckett's *Waiting for Godot* (Grove, 1954). It is not easy reading, a bleak and absurdist depiction of the godless universe in which two characters, Didi and Gogo, two halves of a nonentity, meet each evening to wait for the Answer to It All—which/who, of course, never shows up. They are a mockery of the theological myth that claims there must be a purpose and direction to human life. If there is no God, there is no purpose, except for the games we make up for ourselves to kill time before time kills us. Each evening, Didi and Gogo meet Pozzo and Lucky, who unlike themselves make progress, in a circle. They are the reductio ad absurdum of our ideas of success: the arrogant world-beater and the mouther of empty scholarship. All four indict intelligence and hope in a godless universe. (Don't be too proud to buy the *Cliff's Notes.* They are good teachers when you have no other.)

Shamelessly, I would recommend a book of my own: *Meeting the Living God* (Paulist, 1984). It's sold 85,000 copies, and I've taught it to about 120 groups and still can't wait each day to get back to the classroom and use it to kick the stuffings out of my students' unexamined certitudes, so I make no apologies for it. It begins with epistemology and what we can trust and shows that our ability to see—and therefore to do—the truth is hamstrung by all kinds of brainwashing propaganda systems. It attempts to show the limits of logic, the evidence for and against the existence of God—and how our lives ought to change consistent with our belief about that fact. It concludes with a study of what we can learn of God's nature and personality, from the Artist's handiwork (the universe and people), from other religions, from Judaism, and from Jesus Christ.

❝Unless you've entertained the possibility that God does not exist, you don't choose to believe in God freely.❞

If Scripture, like the language, symbols, and myths in Shakespeare, is so dense and foreign to me, how can I learn to read it without a teacher? The very best I know is *The Jerome Biblical Commentary* (Prentice-Hall, 1968), with articles on topics like modern methods of understanding the Bible, the modes of Jewish thought, and so forth, and the best scholarly understanding of every verse from Genesis through Apocalypse. Very thorough but heavy going for a beginner. To understand how the Bible uses forms meaningful to Jews but not easily accessible to us, try a fun introduction, Lohfink, *The Bible: NOW I Get It!* (Doubleday, 1979). For the Old Testament, begin with Link, *These Stones Will Shout* (Tabor Publishing, 1983), and for the New Testament, O'Malley, *How the Gospels Work* (Paulist, 1980).

Relating to God

The most difficult insight into our relationship with God is the Job insight: how could a good God allow the innocent to suffer; how could God invent death? Parochialized as we are in a time-space understanding, we expect God to meet us on our terms. We mouth the cliché that "God's ways are not our ways," then turn around and expect God to meet us person-to-Person in terms of (our) justice, as if our Maker were answerable to us. The problem of yielding control to God goes all the way back to Adam and Eve.

Nonetheless, it is a truth we can't help gnawing on— standing at the coffin of a seventeen-year-old, watching the slow erosion of our aging parents, reading the latest on the starving in Africa—or on our own streets. We can cocoon ourselves from the seeming injustice of God most of the time, but the inequality and seeming unfairness relentlessly return. The best books I know giving clues to an understanding of the Job question, the Ivan Karamazov question, are Lewis, *The Problem of Pain* (Macmillan, 1962) and Kreeft, *Making Sense Out of Suffering* (Servant, 1986). Kreeft examines insights into suffering from the vantage points of philosophers, artists, prophets, and Jesus, and refuses to accept the easy way out offered by Rabbi Harold Kushner in the far more popular *When Bad Things Happen to Good People:* letting God off the hook by denying divine omnipotence. Adult Christians must come to realize that it is perfectly all right to get good-and-mad at God, as long as we forgive, as with any friend who had betrayed our trust, because of the good times.

When I was a child, I prayed like a child, and I continued to pray like a child until I was long past thirty. I prayed to change God's mind rather than trying to understand God's mind—or at least yielding to it, contenting myself that, no matter what God asked, Someone was with me, struggling through it. I learned to let God manipulate me, rather than the other way round. What cracked the childishness of my praying was the three years that I said Mass every day for no other intention but that God would let my mother die. And I was refused. I'd given God my whole life; oh, I'd stolen a few pears now and then, but I'd given God the whole tree.

And all my giving didn't "pay off" when I really needed it to. Then, in a typically oblique answer to my prayers, God threw in my path Johnston's *Christian Zen* (Harper & Row, 1981), which showed me that, even in my praying, I was trying to dominate God rather than yielding. It gave me ways to let go, center myself, allow God to come into my inner self and manipulate my thoughts. I grew up when I was willing to become a child.

---

66 The problem of yielding control to God goes all the way back to Adam and Eve. 99

Why Be Christian/Catholic?

Just as most of us didn't "choose" to believe in God after an honest look at the alternative but rather just "stuck with God," most of us stayed with the Catholic Church simply because it was our "family," our "tribe," and its customs became as much a part of who we are as our ethnicity or our allergies.

Perhaps the best way to understand the allure of Christianity, "brand-new again," is through biographies: Newman's *Apologia* or Merton's *Seven Storey Mountain.* When one is trying to convert or reconvert a long-baptized adult (or youngster), the stories of those who were atheists or agnostics but found themselves inexorably drawn back not only to belief in God but to the need for an organized, institutional expression of that belief show us the way home, too. Although it is dated in some ways, Chesterton's *Orthodoxy* (Doubleday, 1959) is, in my opinion, still the best way to understand the contradiction of the "solitary Christian." Another is Lewis, *Mere*

Christianity (Macmillan, 1960), and even more accessible, DiGiacomo and Walsh, *Going Together: The Church of Christ* (Seabury, 1978).

If pastors can find even a core group of parents to engage in common study, that "remnant" group would understand, experientially, why it is better to be Christian together than alone. And it might be kind of fun one evening to see the video of *Mass Appeal* and share the insights it provokes.

God and My Relationships

Every relationship between two human beings is a moral relationship, because morality is—pure and simple—understanding how human beings can legitimately deal with one another and with their common environment. Many lifelong Catholics (and, I can testify, almost all their children) believe that Christianity and morality are coterminous. If that were true, all good Jews and Muslims and atheists would be Christian. Christianity does not ask us merely to be un-bad; Christianity asks us to be saints. It raises our motivation from the level of the justice imposed by our shared humanity and our shared moral ecology to a level of loving concern and involvement with the physically and spiritually needy. A genuine Christian has a two-edged motive for solicitude; he or she sees not only a fellow human in need (as any good Jew or Muslim or atheist would) but also Jesus Christ in need, embodied in that person: "I was hungry; I was thirsty . . . ."

Understanding sexual relationships is probably the thorniest moral question for parents of adolescents. Against them stands all the power of television and the rock subculture that pervade almost every waking moment of a child's life outside school and that consistently and effectively make the case for self-absorbed sexuality: "Everybody does it! . . . If it feels good, why not? . . . It's the only way to express love." And many parents are left with the only countermotive they themselves were given for abstinence: not moral integrity but pregnancy. But kids believe the pill has completely eliminated that motive. What now?

> **66Christianity does not ask us merely to be un-bad; Christianity asks us to be saints. 99**

Psychologist Robert Johnson has three small books *He, She,* and *We* (Perennial, 1977) that give an easily understandable insight into the psychology of males, females, and romantic love, using Greek and medieval myths. Bruno Bettelheim's *The Uses of Enchantment* (Vintage, 1977) does the same for Grimm's fairy tales, showing the age-old truth, for instance, that although Snow White was physically ready for her prince at an early age, she was not psychologically ready and had to await her time in her crystal coffin.

One of the best books I've seen to motivate boys to mature treatment of sexuality (if you don't mind a bit of cornball humor) is Bausch, *Becoming a Man* (Twenty-Third Publications, 1988). A more taxing book on the psychology of women is Belenky et al., *Women's Ways of Knowing* (Basic, 1986) or Carol Gilligan, *In a Different Voice* (Harvard, 1982). And Gasiorowski, *Adolescent Sexuality and Sex Education* (Brown, 1988) is an exhaustive study of the entire question.

Continued religious learning is essential not only for parents to assume their obligation as the primary educators of their children, but for the parents themselves to continue to grow as adult Christians; if you're not growing, you're beginning to atrophy. But also it's exhilarating! I can practically guarantee parents will find themselves saying, right out loud, "Aha! So *that's* what that means!" And the best part will be that you found it for yourself and therefore can never lose it.

I never really learned the matter of a course until years after I'd barely passed it, not until I found a need to use the material and went back finally to *understand* it, rather than merely know it. Our children's abrasive questions are just such a providential need: to understand the faith as an adult, in order to lead our young into Christian adulthood. It is actually an invitation from God, to a new Pentecost!

Other Books by William J. O'Malley, S.J.

MEETING THE LIVING GOD
THE FIFTH WEEK
A BOOK ABOUT PRAYING
THE ROOTS OF UNBELIEF
SCRIPTURE AND MYTH
HOW THE GOSPELS WORK
THE VOICE OF BLOOD
PHOENIX
LOVE AND JUSTICE
WHY NOT?